The
Ten
Commandments
of
Good
Teaching

The
Ten
Commandments
of
Good
Teaching

Vickie Gill

CORWIN PRESS, INC.
A Sage Publications Company
Thousand Oaks, California

For information:

Corwin Press, Inc.
A Sage Publications Company
2455 Teller Road
Thousand Oaks, California 91320
E-mail: order@corwinpress.com

SAGE Publications Ltd.
6 Bonhill Street
London EC2A 4PU
United Kingdom

SAGE Publications India Pvt. Ltd.
M-32 Market
Greater Kailash I
New Delhi 110 048 India

Printed in the United States of America

Library of Congress Cataloging-in-Publication Data

Gill, Vickie.
    The ten commandments of good teaching / by Vickie Gill.
        p.   cm.
    ISBN 0-8039-6720-9 (cloth : acid-free paper). — ISBN 0-8039-6721-7 (pbk. : acid-free paper)
    1. Effective teaching.   I. Title.
LB1025.3.G45 1997
371.102—dc21   97-45274

This book is printed on acid-free paper.

    99   00   01   02   03   10   9   8   7   6   5   4   3

Production Editor: S. Marlene Head
Editorial Assistant: Kristen L. Gibson
Typesetters: Laura A. and William C. E. Lawrie
Cover Designer: Marcia M. Rosenburg

Contents

Foreword

There is something different about this book: It is useful—really useful. This is not to derogate other books of the genre; there are many good, useful books that can help you over one kind of hurdle or another. However, Vickie Gill is easy to identify with because she speaks plainly and simply of the everyday realities of teaching. If you have been a teacher of difficult-to-reach, difficult-to-teach students, you will find yourself right here in these pages. You will find the real you: the fulfilled, the frustrated, the puzzled, the angry, the grateful. You will find all of your students here, too: the good, the bad, the unbearable, the unforgettable.

Most "help for the teacher" books are grounded in a philosophy—or perhaps more accurately, they espouse one point of view or another concerning behavior and learning. Mrs. Gill's work is grounded in an honest love for teaching and for children, a sense of calling that reminds us why we teach, and the understanding that even a great teacher needs a plan. Rooted in hard-nosed experience and tempered by logic and kindness, hers is a teaching philosophy that is one part behavior modification, one part child psychology, and one part divine inspiration.

Most teachers cope. They use a variety of tactics borrowed from a variety of authors and professors they had in college. When it comes to dealing with behavior problems, the most commonly taught learning theory is behavior modification. This approach has undergone many evolutions, starting with the highly mechanistic operant conditioning model. Teachers wore wrist counters, and they took data on prebehaviors, the behavior itself, and the consequences of the behavior. Properly implemented, this was a very effective approach. *Properly implemented* is the phrase to focus on. It turns out that it is very difficult to manage such techniques in the hurly-burly of interacting with large groups of students for long periods of time. These techniques have proven so burdensome and difficult that it is extremely rare to find teachers who can devise individual behavior modification programs, implement them, and take data to demonstrate effectiveness and make revisions. They constantly adapt and modify, searching for the best way to put out their brushfires.

What is a better option? Well, let's revisit behavior modification and see what its latest evolutionary form looks like. It looks like common sense made systematic. It looks like clearly defined roles and expectations for students. It looks like a simple system of classroom management and an empathetic, personal style of teacher-student interaction. It looks exactly like Vickie Gill's classroom. She has been on every side of the education dynamic: rebellious student, overwhelmed new teacher, potential burnout victim, and now master teacher. She speaks with the passionate voice of the true believer.

Full of tactics and techniques, straightforward and interesting, this book is loaded with good examples drawn from Mrs. Gill's own trials and errors, but its best contribution may be the expression of a mind-set for successful teachers. It is a mind-set of dedication, empowerment, and positivity that can help fulfill the promise of a teaching career.

Even though I was one of Vickie's professors, I have always learned something when I visited her classroom. And even though her classmates in graduate school were also master teachers, they all acknowledged that they learned from her as well. So will you. Read and enjoy.

JAMES R. LENT
Professor Emeritus
Vanderbilt University

Preface

Except for the 7 years I took off to be a full-time mom, I have been teaching high school students how to read, write, and think since 1972. I love my job. If we could afford it, I'd do it for free. So it always distresses me when each year I encounter an increasing number of new teachers who are ready to quit the profession after a couple of months or experienced teachers who are literally enduring until retirement. Their frustration and misery are passed directly on to their students.

I find I spend a great deal of time defending the teaching profession and giving advice to help struggling teachers succeed. Last summer, I decided to sit down and organize what I know to be true about good teaching into ten basic attitudes—commandments, if you will. Much of what I know I learned through mistakes and failures. One of the wonders of our profession is that teachers get a chance to review and renew at the beginning of every semester. I don't believe that I necessarily know all of the answers; I just haven't been afraid to ask the questions.

This book is designed to give new teachers the tools and courage to follow their best instincts about what to do in their own classrooms. It's also dedicated to experienced teachers who are on the edge of burnout to help them remember what made them want to be teachers in the first place.

If you're good at it, teaching is the best job in the world. If you're not good at it, it's a nightmare that will affect your mental and physical health. This book is not for those who go into teaching to have their summers free or because they think being a teacher will give them the power they lack in other areas of their lives. This book is for those who fell in love with teaching because they love children, and because they truly believe they can positively affect a child's life.

VICKIE GILL
Ashland City, Tennessee
October, 1997

About the Author

Vickie Gill has taught high school English, reading, and journalism since 1972. She has a B.A. in English from San Jose State University and an M.Ed. from Vanderbilt University. Mrs. Gill has won several teaching and community service honors, including Cheatham County Teacher of the Year and Most Innovative Program from the Private Industry Council of Tennessee. She has presented workshops to Middle Tennessee teachers on classroom discipline, school-to-work transitions, and curriculum development. A native Californian, she currently lives with her songwriter husband in a small town outside of Nashville, Tennessee. Her three daughters are graduates of the local public school system and are attending colleges in Tennessee on full scholarships.

To Doug, my constant source;
to Delaney, Jenny, and Casey, my validation;
and to my family and friends, my foundation.

1

Thou Shalt Have
a Calling to Teach

*Education is what survives when what has been
learnt has been forgotten.*

B. F. SKINNER

By any means necessary.

MALCOLM X

I became a teacher because I detested school—hated just about
every minute of it, particularly from sixth grade on. By the
time I was in eighth grade I had a chair of my own right outside the
vice-principal's office. I was a teacher's nightmare—the one in the
back of the class making noises and comments to make the kids
around me laugh. I constantly asked the dreaded question, "Why
do we have to learn this junk anyway?" My teachers would warn
me not to get smart with them, which always struck me as a con-
tradiction in terms. I would read every book on the suggested
reading lists sent home by my English teachers, but I refused to admit that I'd read the books. I didn't want to give them the satisfac-
tion of thinking that they had taught me something. I hiked my
skirts up, ratted my hair, and sported heavy black eyeliner and

white lipstick. When the vice-principal would pull me into her office to wash my face, unroll my skirts, and comb out my hair, I'd march to the closest restroom and redo the whole thing. I was one of the girls who wouldn't let you into the bathrooms at lunch because my friends and I were in there smoking.

In my junior year of high school, my counselor called me in to "discuss my future," one of his minimum job requirements. This man had never taken any notice of me before other than to make big circles around my chair outside the vice-principal's door. He sat me in his office, winced as he perused my rather thick disciplinary file, sighed, and asked me what I planned to do when I grew up. I smiled and told him I was going to be a teacher. He laughed, looked me dead in the eye, and said, "You'll *never* be a teacher." I got up, leaned over his desk, and said, "You don't know me," and walked out of his office.

I understood early on that I was not teaching a subject, I was teaching people.

I'd known I was going to be a teacher since I was 5 years old—it was the only thing I'd ever wanted to do. Even when I was acting out in school, causing a couple of teachers to reconsider their chosen profession, I knew teaching was one of the reasons I was put on this earth. Luckily for me, I had parents who never questioned my goals even when I was at my most rebellious. Because I hated to sit still and listen to lectures, I volunteered to work in Sunday school classes from a very early age, and I knew I had a knack for working with kids. But the main thing that helped me in becoming the teacher I am was all of the horrible or ineffectual teachers I observed. I knew there had to be a better way, so I built my teaching career around engaging the students who hated school the most. In my classes, my students are rewarded for asking,

"Why do we have to learn this stuff?" This shows that they are concerned with their education.

I understood early on that I was not teaching a subject, I was teaching people. I believe my attitude toward school would have been very different if I'd had even one teacher try to figure out why I was acting like such a jerk. I was obviously intelligent, but they settled for stamping all of my report cards with the phrase "not working up to potential." Not one of them ever asked why. If they had, I would have told them that I didn't see the usefulness or the joy in anything they were teaching. It seemed like a complete waste of time to me—one of my teachers even said that high school was a holding zone to keep us teens from glutting the job market. Also, most of my teachers believed that students needed to be controlled with a heavy hand, never really understanding the true nature of power.

I did the bare minimum of what was required to get out of high school and paid for my obstinacy by having to attend a junior college for 2 years. But college was a revelation for me. The teachers didn't care whether I showed up for class because I was paying for the privilege. Suddenly, my education became my own. Every class, every credit was one step closer to my goal, and I blossomed in this atmosphere. Even though it was a painful time for me (and my teachers), my public school experience served me very well in that it taught me what *not* to do as a teacher. For the past 20 years, I've tried to design classes that I would like to attend, and it's made all the difference to me and my students.

Sometimes I want to write my teaching salary off on my income tax forms as a charitable contribution. It's a huge mistake to get into teaching for the money or because you'll have your summers free. I've known teachers like that over the years, and they spend the money and the summers trying to get over the physical and psychological stress the students put them through. I believe you should become a teacher if you'd do it anyway for free. It's one of the hardest jobs I know, requiring you to act as a gifted academician, psychologist, detective, magician, technician, supervisor, entertainer, and counselor all within a class period, then do it all over again. My favorite thing about teaching is that it stimulates both my creative and practical impulses. I also love that I am solely responsible for the quality of what goes on in my classroom. As you probably have figured out already, I have some serious issues with authority figures, but as a teacher I am the authority and solely responsible for the quality of what goes on in my classroom.

I consider teachers to be among an elite
group of people who can truly change
the world.

Teaching is the greatest of all professions. I consider teachers to be among an elite group of people who can truly change the world. I call it the ripple effect. A while back, I was sitting around talking with a group of people who were in college in the early 1970s—a time of tremendous social upheaval and change. We were laughing about the protest marches, the campus takeovers, the hubristic attitude that by handing out leaflets, the world would slap its collective forehead and shout, "Of course you're right—why didn't I think of peace and love and feeding the children?!" Instead, even after toppling an administration, it was business as usual. One person in the group shook his head at what naive fools we'd been, noting that not one of us had followed an idealistic path. I told him that I had—I'd become a teacher and that instead of trying to change thousands of minds at once, I was influencing people daily in a much smaller arena. And possibly my students would raise their children with slightly different attitudes about racism and sexism and their responsibility to the communities in which they live. It's like dropping a pebble in a pool—I can't change everything, but I can help my students to at least examine why they believe what they do and to live a more deliberate life.

————•✦——◆——✦•————

*You're a closely watched role model
who communicates more by what you
do than by what you say.*

————•✦——◆——✦•————

If teaching were easy, anyone could do it. Teachers bear an awesome responsibility because a casual comment by a teacher will become part of a student's life script. How many times have you heard adults say that a teacher's encouragement influenced them to change the course of their lives? On the other hand, I know several adults who speak bitterly of a teacher who told them in third grade that they were stupid or untalented or a waste of time, and they have never forgotten it. As a teacher, you're not allowed to have such a bad day that you would take it out on your students. As a teacher, you're a closely watched role model who communicates more by what you do than by what you say. As a teacher, you will be remembered forever—*how* is up to you. It's an incredibly important and demanding job, and it requires a profound commitment. The first commandment of good teaching? Thou shalt not become a teacher unless you feel a calling to this mother of all professions. Depending on your talent and disposition, it can be the best or the worst way to earn your living.

2

Thou Shalt Demonstrate the Joy of Learning

My husband is a songwriter, so I often attend parties or showcases with people who are not in the field of education. For a long while, I dreaded the moment when someone would ask me what I did for a living, because the minute I said I was a teacher, people's attitudes would change. Either their eyes would glaze over and they would suddenly notice a long-lost friend across the room, or they would straighten their postures, shift uncomfortably, and hide their cigarettes behind their backs. If I foolishly added that I was an English teacher, all conversation would sputter to a painful end. I realized that the general population's impression was that all teachers are judgmental, anal-retentive control freaks who would somehow deduct points at a cocktail party for poor grammar. There were some who would stay to talk, complimenting me on sacrificing my life to such a thankless job. It got so annoying that I developed my own defense mechanisms. Sometimes I would make a joke and say something like, "That's right, I ain't gonna tolerate no bad grammar at this here party." Other times I would thank the person for reducing me to a stereotype and move on. But the easiest thing to do was to sidestep the question and avoid mentioning teaching at all. What's wrong with this picture? I honestly love my job and am tremendously proud of what I do.

Why do people have the impression that teaching is a boring, joyless profession? Maybe it's because they've all been in boring, joyless classes. I have three daughters who spent 12 years in the public school system. I watched them evolve from ravenous learners to bored participants, fulfilling the minimum requirements to maintain their class rankings. When they were little, they were interested in everything—learning was not compartmentalized, labeled, or evaluated. It was just what they did naturally. When they entered school, they quickly realized that acting average and going along with the program was the easiest way to survive. For the most part they were put in rows, handed worksheets, and rewarded for not asking why. Their main goal was to move through the system as quickly as possible to get on with "real life." These were very bright young ladies with a lot of self-control—imagine how painful school is for the kids with learning disabilities or behavior problems.

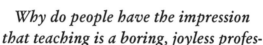

Why do people have the impression that teaching is a boring, joyless profession? Maybe it's because they've all been in boring, joyless classes.

But along the way, all of my girls had a few remarkable teachers who stood out like beacons in a dense fog. What was different about these people? I believe it was that they clearly demonstrated and protected the joy of learning. Their classes were designed for success, accommodated differences, and gave the impression that magic could break out at any moment. These teachers obviously loved students, saw them as individuals, and delighted in their uniqueness. These teachers never stopped learning themselves and would share with their students some new discovery or insight that had delighted or amazed. These teachers made learning so exciting that the students didn't want to stay home for fear of missing out on something really great. These teachers loved what they did, and the students knew it.

I think that one of the hardest things about being a teacher is that we are constant role models. The students watch everything we do, and that can be exhausting. Teaching has a great deal in common with acting and sales. It's not enough that we are completely knowledgeable in the subjects we teach, we also have to make the students want to buy what we're offering. One of the biggest arguments I had with a colleague was over whether or not a teacher needed to motivate his students. This teacher felt that the students should come to him predisposed to learn—that was their job. His job was to disseminate the information. I told him that the administration would be happy to hear about that attitude because if that was all that was required of him, we could pass out textbooks, put on a videotape of him at his best, and fire his sorry self, thus saving the school system thousands and thousands of dollars over the years.

Take time to remember what drew you to teaching in the first place. What kinds of things did your favorite teachers do?

One of the most useful things you can do as a teacher is take time to remember what drew you to teaching in the first place. What kinds of things did your favorite teachers do? What made you fall in love with the subject you teach? What was the atmosphere and set-up of your favorite class? Which lessons made an impression on you? What was useful for you later in your life? Then you have to monitor yourself over the years to be sure you are including these joyful experiences in your own lessons.

Another tremendous advantage is to remember what it is like to be a kid. A few years ago, I was sitting in an inservice with around 50 other teachers from my school district. The presenter asked the teachers to think back to two of the most significant memories they had of high school. He then asked the group how many of these memories happened inside the classroom. Not one hand went up. Many of us noted that the things that really mattered to us in school were the ball games, social events, broken hearts, cliques, fights, and awards. Most of what we learned academically had been long forgotten unless it was in the subject we were currently teaching.

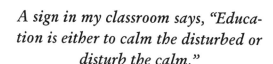

A sign in my classroom says, "Education is either to calm the disturbed or disturb the calm."

I have a sign up in my classroom that says, "Education is either to calm the disturbed or disturb the calm." This has profoundly affected the way I teach. I discuss this saying with my classes on the first day of school, asking them to decide whether they would classify themselves as among the calm or among the disturbed. This usually creates a lively discussion, and I get some immediate insights into some of my students. I point out that many of them have drifted through school for years, sitting quietly, doing whatever was required, questioning nothing, and waiting for the bell to ring. These are the calm and my job is to disturb them—I need to make them take charge of their own education, analyzing information rather than just regurgitating it. I work with them in small groups so that there is no hiding in the back of the class and everyone has to defend an answer. I let them know that my class will have a great tolerance for differences of opinion, but everyone must have an opinion and be able to back it up. Then I address the "disturbed." These are the students who have what I call "noisy minds." It could be that their personal life is in such chaos that they feel nothing the school has to offer could be of any use. Others are extremely bright students who have become openly hostile to the mediocrity of most classwork. My job is to show them how the skills I'm teaching can help them take control of their lives and their futures. My job is to make them think something they have never thought before. My job is to help them turn down the noise in their minds so that they can concentrate on the academic skills that will make them successful.

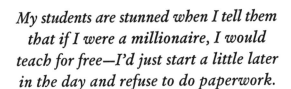

My students are stunned when I tell them that if I were a millionaire, I would teach for free—I'd just start a little later in the day and refuse to do paperwork.

Sometimes I want to thank the few really terrible teachers in my school because they make my work so much easier. They spend so much of their time boring, humiliating, or trying to control the students that when the kids get to me, it's like a breath of fresh air. To many students, my class is a safe, exciting, authentic learning environment where mistakes and handicaps are just useful information. My students are stunned when I tell them that if I were a millionaire, I would teach for free—I'd just start a little later in the day and refuse to do paperwork. Quite often, I'm one of the few adults they know who loves her work. I use this as a launching pad for a unit on goal making. I try to get them to focus on their calling—on what gives them joy—and try to help them figure out how to make a living at it.

Every year, I have several students who laugh when I tell them that money should not be a deciding factor in picking a career. They are quite straightforward in pointing out what a sucker I am to settle for a teacher's pay. Last year, one senior told me that if it paid enough, he'd be willing to do anything. I suggested that if he were offered one job doing something he loved for $15 an hour and another job doing something he hated for $30 an hour, he'd be a fool to take the higher-paying job. He laughed and said that if the pay was good, he didn't care what they wanted him to do. It took only a couple of minutes to completely change his mind. I asked him to think about the class in school that he had hated the most—the one that he thought he'd never get through because it was so boring and the teacher was so awful. Then I told him I'd pay him $30 an hour to sit in that class all day every day for the next 30 years. That got his attention. How could a person who got into teaching because of the love of a subject or a desire to help the young people in our country design a class that was so abhorrent that this student would cut his life-long pay in half to avoid it?

Human beings are born to learn. Babies do it so naturally it's almost impossible to keep them from it. Ask a group of kindergartners about their future plans and they shout out an eclectic set of goals involving a career as a singer-doctor-astronaut-veterinarian-preacher-mommy-on-the-side. Ask a group of high school students what they want to do for a living and it's likely that the majority of them will shrug their shoulders and mutter, "I don't know." What happened in those 12 years? The second commandment of good teaching? Thou shalt protect and demonstrate the joy of learning.

3

Thou Shalt Keep
Your Eyes on the Prize

Now that I've tried to inspire you with the best that teachers can be, just how do you create such a class? How do you choose what to teach? I once had a graduate class where the instructor asked the question, "What's worth knowing?" The class was full of teachers working on master's degrees, and I could tell many of them felt that this was a stupid question. But I found it exhilarating. It really caused me to examine what I was teaching. Earlier I mentioned getting into trouble in a class for asking why we had to learn what the teacher was presenting. To me, that should be the most significant question the teacher addresses. If you plan to design your class around the state's prepared curriculum, then be sure you have an answer to that question. And the following answers are not OK: (a) Your teacher next year will expect you to know this; (b) Because I told you so; (c) You'll be asked this material on a test; (d) This is what every class at this level is studying; (e) It's none of your business; or (f) I had to suffer through this, so should you.

Recently, I asked four honor students who excelled in their advanced math classes to tell me how they might use what they'd learned. The best answer I got was that they may need it later on in life. Not one of them could tell me how they would use all of these math facts even though all of them were glad they'd taken the classes. I think the reason that so little of what students study in school stays with them is that no one has demonstrated the usefulness of the information. My husband uses geometry and algebra to design decks, but he admits that when he was learning those skills in high school, he had no idea that they could be applied to construction. In my experience, I never really learned anything until I had to use it. Good teachers provide practical applications for the facts they're presenting so that they're preparing their students to be more than great Trivial Pursuit players.

I never really learned anything until I had to use it. Good teachers provide practical applications for the facts they're presenting.

Whenever I design the curriculum for a class, I always ask myself what I want the students to be able to do when they leave the class. In other words, I start from the big picture then work backward. If I want them to be able to write a college-level research paper, I break that objective down into all of the skills they'll need to accomplish it. If I want them to know how to communicate effectively on a job, I brainstorm on everything I can think of that will promote that skill.

Another question I ask my students on the first day of class is, "What are the characteristics of an educated person?" We toss around ideas for a while, and I write all of their responses on the board. Usually, they'll say things like having a big vocabulary or having read Shakespeare is a sign of an educated person. I always ask if being able to fix a car's engine or designing a house would label a person "educated." After much dissension, I try to lead them to consider these three attributes: (a) Educated people can go find out what they need to know, (b) educated people share a common body of knowledge with other educated people that aids them in finding out what they need to know, and (c) educated people are curious—they are lifelong learners. When I break it down to its simplest form, these are my three main teaching goals. Of course these are huge, especially when students enter my class completely uninterested in finding out anything, with an uncommonly small body of knowledge, and with a real distaste for learning. But it's a starting place.

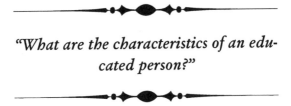

"What are the characteristics of an educated person?"

Another sign in my room says, "If you find what is within you, what you find will save you; if you do not find what is within you, what you do not find will destroy you." Many of the lessons I teach throughout the year are designed to help the students discover what it is they were meant to do. I know this sounds beyond the realm of what schools should be required to do, but until the student focuses on some personal goals, most of what he or she does in your class will be forgotten after the final exam.

I'm blessed because I teach English—the greatest of all subjects because it involves reading, writing, and thinking. These three skills are so flexible that I can create a curriculum to address almost any need my students may have. For example, I begin every semester with a unit on goal making. This allows me to get a pretest on their writing skills by having them write a composition about their plans for the next 10 years. This gives me a pretty accurate picture of the students' writing abilities and the kind of work they will need to do to reach their goals. It also sets up a high-interest discussion for the first small-group meetings. The really focused students can share their plans, and the clueless can start to consider some options. During this unit, the students will complete a computer program that suggests possible careers based on the students' responses to questions about their interests, skills, and plans. This software program will also give up-to-date information about job requirements, salaries, training, and availability. It includes a database of colleges throughout the state and information about getting into those colleges. We do all sorts of personality and interest analysis sheets, constantly trying to match each student to a career. The students will write letters to colleges researching financial aid and admission requirements. We have speakers from various businesses who tell the students about their jobs and, more important, about what they expect from their employees. The point is that none of the work done throughout this unit is busywork. The students see the usefulness of everything they do, discover the power of the written word through letters, and learn how to tackle the puzzle of their futures.

The only adults in the world who will be asked to identify nouns and verbs are English teachers.

I know that most of the curriculum frameworks that you can get from the state department start with big goals that are then broken down into objectives. But quite often, teachers get so focused on moving through the objectives, they lose sight of the big picture. When I began teaching in Tennessee, the English Department chairperson and I heatedly disagreed over what should be taught in a high school English class. She insisted that I should be working from the state-adopted grammar and literature textbooks, moving through the objectives in exactly the same time frame as the other English teachers. I pointed out to her that it was not unusual for me to have students in my senior English class who had done precious little writing because of this inflexible focus on the parts rather than the whole. She countered that the students had to master the basic grammatical skills before they could possibly hope to write a composition. I asked her how she thought a baby should be taught to walk. Should we put the child in a high chair and show him diagrams of the leg, requiring him to memorize the names of all of the moving parts? Should we show the baby films of people walking? Or should we put the baby on the floor and let her stumble and fall and stumble and fall until one day she stays up? This is exactly what we do when we teach writing.

Moving ahead to the big picture, the only adults in the world who will be asked to identify nouns and verbs are English teachers. Everyone else will just unconsciously use those parts of speech. The students need to write and write and write some more. They need to write letters that are really mailed and compositions that analyze their opinions. They need to read articles about marriage and parenting and write responses describing what they will do in these relationships. This is not only high interest but essential to their futures. I further annoyed this colleague by pointing out that if I ever needed to take a year off from teaching, for whatever reason, I'd just pass out the grammar books, give a 15-minute lecture on nouns and verbs, then have them do problems 1-50 at the end of the chapter while I kick back at my desk. There is so little time and so much to do within a class period that we must focus on the most effective methods available. If a student has been working in grammar and spelling texts for 10 years and still doesn't get it, then this is an ineffectual use of time and we should try something else.

Choosing goals on the first day of a semester forces the students to take responsibility for what will go on in my class.

I need to tell you at this point that I do teach to tests. In my reading/writing labs, I have students who will not graduate from high school unless they pass the state competency test. But I make this their choice. On the first day of a semester, I pass out a sheet with a long list of goals—things I can teach relating to reading, writing, and thinking. One of the goals is to pass the competency test. I then ask the students to put a check next to all of the things they'd like to tackle during this semester. Finally, I have them go back and circle the three goals that are the most important to them. I believe this accomplishes two things. One, it tells me what my students think they need to know. I can group students with common goals. Two, it forces the students to take responsibility for what will go on in my class. It gives them a sense of ownership and a sense that they are not empty vessels into which I will pour whatever I think they need.

You'll be amazed at how focused this makes them—and how uncomfortable. Some of the students don't want to admit that they are in school to learn anything at all. They see it as a holding zone, keeping them from enjoying "real life." Last year, I passed out the goal sheets to a group of 9th, 10th, and 11th graders in my reading lab. When I went around the room picking up the sheets, one boy handed me a blank sheet of paper—nothing but his name on top. He looked at me defiantly, hoping for his first skirmish to establish the battle lines. Instead, I glanced at the paper, gazed at him fondly, and murmured, "This is wonderful." He shifted uncomfortably and said, "What do you mean?" I smiled and answered that by not checking anything he was telling me that he wanted to learn everything and that he was my favorite kind of student. I told him I appreciated his confidence in me and that I'd do everything I could to help him succeed. He eyed me suspiciously for a while, but he was mine for the rest of the class.

Preparing for the state competency test is extremely boring for both the teacher and the students. However, when it's their choice, it adds a new energy and dedication to the pursuit of this goal. Because the testing takes place about 6 weeks after the semester begins, I make this an intensive, all-out attack, with the promise of the much more interesting reading, writing, and thinking activities after the test is over. Imagine—reading and writing and thinking are the rewards to look forward to.

A few years ago, one of my supervisors asked to see the objectives for my reading lab for the following year. He called me at home in July and said he needed to see what I would be teaching for a state department form he was completing. I told him that I could not possibly know my objectives until I met my students. This just stunned him, and he accused me of teaching without a plan. I told him I could easily hand him a beautifully sequenced set of objectives lifted straight from the state's curriculum guide for the basic competency test—this would be no problem. But what if, when I met my students in the fall, 90% of them had passed the competency test? What if some of them couldn't read at all? What if some were pretty good writers, but they hated reading? What if some had such severe emotional problems that they couldn't even sit still? I explained to my supervisor that this is why the first week of school is so hectic—I have to find out what my students need before I can create the objectives. However, I did add that my main goal was to turn out educated persons, told him the three characteristics of an educated person, and suggested he could write that on his form.

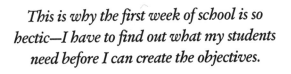

This is why the first week of school is so hectic—I have to find out what my students need before I can create the objectives.

When deciding what to teach, you have to trust your instincts. I can picture several of my former supervisors shifting uneasily in their chairs thinking of those incompetent teachers who show movies all day or let the students sit and talk as long as they leave the teacher alone. My response is that these people are not teachers and should not be in the profession. If someone as incompetent as that has been hired and has maintained his or her job through tenure, then it's the principal's problem to ensure at least that the state guidelines are followed. But it is not the principal's job to tamper with authentic teaching that works. Figure out what you want your students to be able to do when they exit your class, make sure these objectives match what they will need to be successful in life, and pass on that joy of learning that made you choose your subject in the first place. You need to be original and teach in the style that works best for you. The third commandment of good teaching? Thou shalt know where you are going and keep your eyes on the prize.

4

Thou Shalt Be
Organized and Accountable

I'm a big believer in the old saying that luck happens when preparation meets opportunity. Most people who are really good at what they do work really hard, and what I'm about to suggest in this chapter will definitely present a challenge to you. Now that you've captured the vision of what you want to teach—the big picture—the next task is to brainstorm on all of the steps that will take the students to those goals. After that, you need to identify the best ideas, sequence them into teaching units, then plan activities that will demonstrate and promote the skills that the students will need to reach the original goals.

When brainstorming, allow yourself to be completely non-judgmental—no idea is too silly or too difficult. Leave yourself open to everything. I get some of my best teaching ideas in the oddest places. I constantly rip quotes, addresses, or articles out of magazines and newspapers. I subscribe to English and adolescent literacy journals. I tape almost everything I watch on TV so I can stop the program and write down a quote or an idea. I participate in an Internet discussion group about the teaching of reading and writing. I constantly ask people I meet from all walks of life to identify the most useful things they learned in school. I interview employers and personnel directors to find out what they want us to teach in the schools. And I read all types of things to keep up on what is going on the world.

One of the big goals I have for my senior English students is for them to write a college-level research paper on the word processors in my classroom. To get the students ready for this project, I introduce them to the techniques of research through a unit on debate. The first assignment I give is to outline and write a four-paragraph paper presenting both sides of a controversial issue. This allows me to show them how to write an introduction, conclusion, and supporting points, and how to remove themselves from a topic. I quote F. Scott Fitzgerald, who said that a great mind can hold two conflicting thoughts at the same time. I tell the students that they can never really win a debate until they thoroughly understand what the opposition believes. I point out that this skill will serve them well in their relationships at home and on the job. This is amazingly difficult for some of the students but an enlightening experience. After they research the topic and we review their rough drafts, they use the word processors to create a composition without errors.

Meanwhile, I get them ready for an actual debate. The class votes on two or three controversial issues, and I let them sign up for the topic of their choice. The only catch is that they won't know which side of the issue they will be defending until the day before the debate. This is when it gets really interesting and some real learning occurs. Often students are highly opinionated about a number of topics, but they haven't a clue as to what the opposition would say. Sometimes during this activity I can literally see the opening of their minds.

A number of years ago I had a student in my senior English class who was the most overtly racist person I had ever met. His racism ran so deep that when he would say highly offensive things in class, he didn't have that look of defiance sported by most people who are trying to shock. He really believed that the grass was green, the sun was hot, and nonwhites were inferior. He and I had already exchanged some heated sentiments about this during the semester, and when it came time to choose the topics to debate, he raised his hand, smirked at his buddies, and suggested that all blacks should be sent back to Africa. I never missed a beat and wrote his topic on the board with the rest of them. He generated enough support in the class to have his topic voted as one of the three to be debated the following week. He kept waiting for me to argue with him or censor his suggestion, but I just set up the debates as usual. On the day before the debate, the eight students who signed up for his topic gathered before me to draw "for" and "against" slips from a basket on my desk. As luck would have it, he drew an "against" paper. He was furious, but I told him that I had honored his input, and now it was his turn to honor the rules of the debate. Most of his friends predicted that he would not show up the next day, but he was there, he was prepared, and he dazzled the audience. He argued passionately and intelligently for racial harmony and equality, and we were stunned. His team won the debate and he made sure that everyone knew he was just doing it for the grade, but for a moment I know that he at least examined both sides of an opinion he'd never questioned since he was a child. I have no idea if he ever softened his views or changed his actions in any way, but I was extremely proud of him for those 15 minutes, and I believe he will never forget the experience.

I believe that for every objective you choose to teach, you can design meaningful, exciting, and authentic activities to reach your goal.

This debate unit takes about 2 weeks out of the semester, but as you can see, a myriad of valuable skills are practiced in a dynamic atmosphere designed to engage every student. Most of the employers I talk with want us to teach basic reading, writing, math, computer, communication, and teamwork skills. This unit covers everything but math. I believe that for every objective you choose to teach, you can design meaningful, exciting, and authentic activities to reach your goal. In my reading lab, I work with many students who are reading anywhere from 2 to 10 years below their grade level. Some of these students are parents, a few are even married. Because most have some sort of learning disability, it is very likely that they will pass this struggle with the printed word on to their children. So in the course of teaching them to read, I teach them how to teach someone else to read. For example, I have some students who need to review basic phonetic principles, such as short vowel sounds, and this can be humiliating for a 16-year-old. When I begin the class, I tell them that at the end of the semester, we will be going to a primary school three times a week to tutor little K-2 students. Therefore, they need to pay close attention to everything I show them, because they will be assigned a student of their own to teach. This really gets their attention. As I work with the group studying vowel sounds, I also demonstrate to them how to teach their own children to read. After years of working with this cross-age tutoring program, I'm not convinced that my students dramatically raise the reading levels of the primary school children. But I do know that these experiences have raised my students' reading levels and have provided a healthy boost to their self-esteem.

Which brings us to one of the most important parts of good teaching. You must develop a system to document what you do. Every year, I work with students who have received passing grades in all of their English classes as well as the state competency test. The only problem is that they can barely read and write. I don't believe a list of grades is a very useful indicator of a student's progress. As a supplement, I keep a portfolio on each of my students. I know this sounds like just more paperwork, but it's the most accurate way I can demonstrate what a student has accomplished in my class. For example, for my senior English students, each portfolio has a set of pretests (writing, reading comprehension, spelling, listening, goals, etc.). Added to this are several assignments that must be done in class on the word processors and must be perfect. These include a cover letter and a résumé, as well as several typed essays. At the end of the semester, I give each of my students a large envelope containing examples of their early work and their perfect papers, including three copies of their résumés and their corrected research paper. I tell them to stick this envelope in their underwear drawer for safekeeping, because every paper will be useful to them later on in college or when seeking a job. This is amazing to most of them. They often comment that this was the first class in which they could clearly see what they had accomplished and the first class in 12 years that required them to do something again and again until it was perfect.

So how do you keep up with the constant correcting and monitoring that this kind of system requires? My solution is to work with my students in three small groups. The cap on my reading lab is 15 students per class, and I've convinced my administrators to put no more than 25 students in my English classes. My school has adopted the four-period-day schedule, requiring me to teach three classes a day. Each class is 90 minutes long, so I meet with each group for about 25 minutes. As I'm meeting with one group, the second group will be on the computers working on writing, spelling, vocabulary, or career software. The students in the third group are at their seats (tables in my class) working on the assignment they will be bringing up for me to discuss or correct in a few minutes.

I often think that for many of my students, I'm one of the few adults with whom they have a meaningful conversation all day.

This system accomplishes a number of things. First, it creates a very businesslike atmosphere in the class—everyone is working all of the time and a cardinal rule is that the class must be quiet enough so that the group working with me is not disturbed. I often tell the students that if I'm working, you're working, and I teach all period. Second, the small groups create informal settings in which students can take risks and get individual attention from me. Third, I can assign a great deal of writing because I can quickly rotate each student to the chair on my right to review the assignment then and there. We jokingly call my ink pen the "laser pen"—capable of finding errors in anything. But the atmosphere is light and respectful, and I can go over the errors with the students rather than handing back a composition covered with red ink that proves only that the teacher is very good at proofreading. This is when I offer mini-lessons on grammar and structure. Fourth, this is a great way for me to get to know my students as individuals. There is no sense of invisibility in the class, which is what I counted on when I was causing so many disruptions as a teenager. I often think that for many of my students, I'm one of the few adults with whom they have a meaningful conversation all day. Finally, this system largely eliminates the techniques most students have mastered by high school: copying someone else's homework and uncanny peripheral vision. I rarely assign worksheets or questions in the back of a chapter, so I can tell very quickly when someone is trying to pass off another student's work as his or her own.

A few years ago, I worked with a difficult young man who had become very good at passing classes by forcing other students to share homework or test answers. It took a while for me to convince him that (a) I read every word my students write, sometimes several times, and (b) I'm not an idiot. I knew he'd been goofing off on the computers, but when his group came to the board, he turned in a beautiful one-page, double-spaced composition about his career goals. He'd pulled up another student's word processing file, deleted her name, and added his own. Evidently, he'd had several teachers in the past who graded papers by weighing or measuring or something, and he'd been rewarded with passing grades. As I glanced over the paper, I immediately remembered where I'd seen it before, so I pulled the girl's portfolio and both of the students into the hallway. I gave the girl a wink as I pretended to lambaste her for turning in plagiarized work. I purposely didn't look directly at the boy, but I could see his face getting redder and redder as the girl protested her innocence. Finally, he admitted to copying her paper, and I advised him to read enough next time to at least know that his topic sentence was proudly announcing his plans to become a cosmetologist. He became a pretty good worker after that.

To be able to pull this off, you have to be extremely organized. I have daily lesson plans written in pencil just in case they need to be revised. I've designed a chart that shows me at a glance what each group should be doing during the 25-minute sessions. The seat assignments are written on a chalkboard at the back of the class, and the necessary materials are laid out before the day begins. I usually plan in 2-week cycles, giving a vocabulary or spelling test on the 14th day. At this time, the students staple all of their work together in a very specific order using a list of assignments I distribute. Most of the work has been corrected in the small-group meetings, so I quickly average the grades and put one grade in my roll book. On that day, we often have a large-group meeting in which we discuss what we've learned over the past 2 weeks and where we're going in the next 2 weeks. Other than the first week of school, this is the only time I work with the class as a whole. Then, twice a month, I give the students free time during the last 30 to 45 minutes of the period to play the normally forbidden computer games or work on a project of their choice while I correct the tests and record the grades. I used to feel guilty about this unstructured time, but I built it into the system so that I didn't have to stay after school or come in on weekends just to keep up with the grades. It is also one of the few times I can talk casually with the students about personal problems or about what's going on in their lives.

There is always something for the students to do, and they get very individualized attention.

Because I work with the students for only 25 minutes per group, it's very important that I have the full time with them. This system eliminates many behavior problems in that there is always something for the students to do and they get very individualized attention, which increases their chances for success. To give my group my undivided attention, I assign "contact persons" for each group. I do this at the end of the first week because by then it's pretty obvious which students are pretty good with the computers, have reasonable social skills, and can follow instructions. Students who have trouble on the computers or with the seatwork know to quietly ask their contact person before asking me. A vast majority of the problems can be dealt with this way, allowing me to work with my small group undisturbed.

Besides the test and classwork grades, I also put a double participation grade in the roll book every 2 weeks. This is determined by a chart I keep daily that indicates how the students worked during the class period. Each day when the students leave, I quickly mark a plus, a check, or a minus next to their names. A plus means that they worked all period and were prepared when they came to the small group to work with me. A check means I had to speak to them to remind them to get to work or they caused a slight disturbance in the class, but got right back to work. A minus means they had a bad day, getting little done, sleeping, or causing such a disturbance that I had to divert my attention from the small group to deal with their problems. These marks break down into numerical values: plus = 10 points, check = 5 points, and a minus = 0 points, with a possible perfect score of 100. I give this grade a double value because it rewards the students in the class who have poor English skills and really struggle with their classwork and tests but work hard every day to improve. It also challenges the students who come into the class with excellent English skills but who are used to doing only what is necessary to get by. These students can ace a test but waste a tremendous amount of time, usually disturbing other people while they do it. Also, these students will make the worst kinds of employees unless they learn that they will be paid based on their efforts and that their job is to stay busy. Sometimes the kids will come in begging for a free day or a movie or something. I tell them that they've already mastered movie viewing, sitting around talking, and sleeping. In fact, most of them could earn a Ph.D. in those areas. I point out that it would be an insult to them for me to teach objectives they'd already mastered. Let's get to work.

Teaching can eat up your life—it is very possible to spend all day and night in your school trying to help everyone and keeping up with your work.

Getting organized will pay off for you in a number of ways. Your students will have confidence in what you're teaching because you have an agenda and know specifically where you're going. There is always something meaningful to do if you have a substitute. You eliminate a huge percentage of discipline problems because you don't spend the first part of each class scrambling for materials that you forgot to prepare. Also, if parents or administrators have a question about a student's grades or work, you have the documentation at your fingertips. Finally, you will put in less overtime because you've developed a system that works within the given time constraints. Remember that teaching can eat up your life—it is very possible to spend all day and night in your school trying to help everyone and keeping up with your work. You can never give enough. As passionate as I am about my job, I have a life away from the classroom that is equally important and needs to be protected. This not only shields me from burnout, it also makes me a more interesting, well-rounded role model for my students. The fourth commandment of good teaching? Thou shalt be organized and accountable for your students' success.

5

Thou Shalt Ask
and Ye May Receive

Up to this point, I've tried to describe teaching as a visionary's job that will wear you out. You may be ready to shout "Check, please!" and find employment in the recreation and leisure field. But there are ways to make your life a lot easier. The most useful is to figure out specifically the tools you need to do the best job you can and then ask for them. The worst thing that can happen is someone will say no and you'll have to seek elsewhere or modify your plan. But it's been my experience that people will say yes more often than no, and that those who get are those who ask.

It is a good idea to keep an ear to the ground about what's going on elsewhere in the school.

Quite often a colleague will come into my classroom to borrow something or to ask my advice. This is usually a teacher who is struggling with her students. During the course of our conversation, this person will turn around and say, "Well, I could be doing a good job, too, if I had this big room and all of these computers."

Sometimes the comment is designed to make me feel guilty for my wealth, but it doesn't work. I have 10 computers, five printers, a scanner, and a phone line in my room because I asked. They didn't. I'm not so naive as to think that all they need to do is run up to the front office and hand the principal a list of items they want for their classroom. This probably won't work, although I've gotten a number of things I've needed by describing to my principal the really cool project I'm working on that would bring glory and honor to his school, if I only had a certain piece of equipment or if he'd pay to send me to a conference somewhere. I've been taken aback a number of times by how easily the principal has agreed. I will admit that it is a good idea to keep an ear to the ground about what's going on elsewhere in the school, and the bookkeeper or secretaries can be incredibly helpful in choosing the right moment. It also helps if you have proven to be an effective and useful teacher. But the point is that you'll never get what you need unless you ask. "No" is not a rejection, just a detour.

When I was designing my class, I knew that I needed to have enough computers to be able to work with the students in groups. I already had a few that my brother (who works for IBM) had helped me acquire, but they were discontinued models and woefully out of date. One day, I was sitting in a teachers' meeting and the principal was describing a new system the counselors would be using to help students plan for their futures. All eighth graders would be required to choose either a "college prep" track or a "tech prep" track when choosing which classes to take in high school. The goal was to raise the requirements for graduation and eliminate the situation where a student is handed a diploma but is prepared for neither college nor work. The state department was mandating that the schools raise the requirements and quality of all high school classes to avoid the embarrassment of a graduate who could not read his or her diploma.

This great idea gave me a great idea. I wrote up a proposal for a Reading/Writing Lab that would be designed to help students bring their skills up to the point where they could succeed in these more challenging classes. When I presented it to the school board, I emphasized the fact that it would be imprudent to require more from the students without offering support classes to get them up to par. Therefore, I was offering my services as the coordinator of a new reading lab to help ensure a quality education for all graduates. All I needed to accomplish this were some up-to-date computers. The board promised to get back to me, and I held my breath. A few weeks later, the technology coordinator called to say the board had approved my plan and the superintendent wanted to know how many computers I needed. I'd been around the block with this sort of thing before, so I asked for twice as many as I wanted. "Ten," I said. She said, "OK, anything else?" I about fainted, but recovered quickly. "And five printers!" "OK, anything else?" Now I was scrambling. "And software and paper!" She told me she'd get the order right out and the stuff would be delivered to my classroom by the beginning of the school year. I was stunned. They were giving me far more than I expected because I asked.

I was stunned. They were giving me far
more than I expected because I asked.

Later on when I was assigned to teach a journalism class, I was able to get a phone in my room. Few of the teachers in my school have phones, and this has always been a real inconvenience, but it was considered too big an expense to be justified. I went to my principal and told him that my journalism students would need to be selling ads and interviewing people in the community as part of their classwork, and a phone was essential for a class like this. I also pointed out that the yearbook office had a phone. This kind of association can be very useful, which is why it's important to stay aware of what is going on in the rest of the school. It was certainly the deciding factor for me, and a phone line was installed the following week. It's important to note that I wouldn't have become angry if my principal had said no, and I certainly wouldn't have given up. It was just the first step.

Years ago, I read a book called *Games People Play* (1964) by Eric Berne. I found the ideas in this book very useful in dealing with students, teachers, parents, and administrators, even though it was not written specifically for educators. One of the games it describes is called "Wooden Leg." People who play this game always have excuses as to why they can't do something they want or need to do. "I could really teach history if it weren't for these awful kids," or "I'd like to try some more interesting things in my classes if it weren't for the administrators," or "There'd be no stopping me if I could only get the money from the school board," and on and on. It is true that sometimes great ideas are stifled due to lack of funds or support, but I don't believe in making excuses. Either do it or don't, but for heaven's sake, don't whine about it. That not only doesn't help the situation, but it makes you look impotent to the other staff members.

It will save you much wasted effort if you can figure out what is out of your control and then stop worrying about it.

I have a large poster of the famous prayer that reminds us that true wisdom is knowing the difference between the things we can do something about and the things we can't do anything about. I make a whole lesson out of this philosophy with my students. I tell them that they are not victims and that they can choose whether or not to live with a problem. When you're working in a school, it will save you much wasted effort if you can figure out what is out of your control and then stop worrying about it. In the same manner, figure out what is within your control and take some action. Another game described in *Games People Play* is called "Yes, but." It goes like this. Someone comes to you with a problem and you offer several possible solutions. However, after each suggestion, the other person says, "Yes, but . . . " and tells you why he or she can't do that. I will play this game through three "yes, buts," and then I realize that the person does not want to solve the problem, he or she just wants to complain about it. After that, I just listen or move on.

I have a friend who is a firm believer in visualization—physically and mentally creating a very specific image of what it is you want. She believes that when you become this focused, what you need will come to you. It's happened many times in her life. This doesn't mean that you just sit around and wish. Quite often I've stumbled on solutions to problems by mentioning what I need to a wide variety of people. The people who work in schools can be amazingly resourceful, and you'll be surprised at the connections they have outside of the system. Some of the most valuable resources you have available to you are the janitors, maintenance personnel, and secretaries. They know far more than you ever will about what is going on in the school, and they can make your life a lot easier.

Every problem has a solution; sometimes we need to be a little more clever or look at it from a totally different perspective.

Students and parents will also amaze you. Last year, I wanted to build another light table for my journalism class but couldn't find a piece of glass thick enough. I mentioned this to my senior English students and one boy shouted, "My daddy works for Ford Motor—we'll get you that glass!" I've had students bring in printer paper and other office supplies donated by their parents. (I always double-check with their folks to make sure it is "donated.") I've asked parents to speak to classes about their professions, and sometimes they will connect me with someone who works in a field my students are researching. I've also had many useful items donated by community businesses who are glad to support the local schools. I practice what I preach to my students and write letters to anyone who can possibly help me do the best job I can. When a letter is answered, I share it with my students to point out the power of the written word. The worst thing that can happen is that the request is denied.

If you're a new teacher, listen to students, teachers, and other personnel talk about the other teachers in the school. Pretty soon you'll hear someone's name come up over and over because of the interesting things going on in his or her class or because that person is involved in the decision-making processes of the school. Go to this teacher and ask for help. I guarantee that 99% of the time, the teacher will be delighted to share information, materials, and advice. Some schools will have a mentor system in place already, but if your school doesn't, find your own mentor. I've had teachers sit in on my classes during their planning periods to observe the system I've created or to learn how to work with students with learning or behavior problems. This has never bothered me, and I'm honored that they asked. I really believe in being kind and helpful to everyone I can because I know I'll need help myself in the future. Some of the biggest hurdles I've cleared were because I called in favors from people I'd helped in the past. Another resource that has become available in the past few years is the Internet. It's pretty simple to hook up with people who are working in the same field as you and who may have very practical answers to your questions. Every problem has a solution; sometimes we need to be a little more clever or look at it from a totally different perspective. The fifth commandment of good teaching? Ask and ye just may receive.

6

Thou Shalt Be
Fair and Prepared

Now that you have your vision, your lesson plans, and the equipment you need, how in the heck do you get the little hoodlums to sit down and listen to you? I'll be honest—I think discipline is the biggest challenge you'll face in the classroom, and it is surely the Achilles' heel of most new teachers. I've been teaching for many, many years, and you can tell that I love my job. However, when I started out I wanted to quit because I was sure I'd never get the students to behave. It was without a doubt my weakest point. Now I consider it one of my strengths. What happened?

In the beginning, I did not understand the nature of power or control. I had heard all of the advice passed down for generations about not smiling until Christmas, starting out tough but easing up as the class progresses, and treating the kids like they treat you. These gems may work for some people, but they were useless for me. I had two problems at the get-go: (a) I wanted the students to enjoy my class, and (b) I remember what I did as a kid to inflexible control freaks. In my experience, mere force just didn't work. My problem was that the kids would be pretty good for a while, but they would push for more and more freedom, and the class would end in chaos with both of us glad to see the other leave. I often left school in tears and dreaded going back. After a great deal of experience, I realized that I was doing two things wrong. First, the students could tell that I was apologetic that we had to have rules and unsure about what I was doing. Second, I made threats that I didn't back up. The students saw right through me and, human nature being what it is, they wrestled for control of the class. What was interesting was that none of us was very happy about that. This was my first clue: Children like to know there is someone in charge—someone who has their best interests at heart and who has a plan. I grew up hating rules, but I came to realize that there are very few human interactions that can function without them.

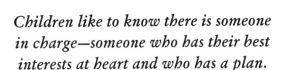

Children like to know there is someone
in charge—someone who has their best
interests at heart and who has a plan.

A while back, one of my reading classes was not going well. Partly due to the mix of students in the class, many of whom had learning and behavioral disabilities, I felt I was spending more time than usual just keeping the kids in line. Instead of placing blame or coming down on the students with an iron fist, I found a solution when I least expected it. I was reading the monthly magazine published by the National Education Association, which focuses on what teachers are doing all across America. In it was a short profile of a history teacher who had a unique way of getting his students to understand the need for laws in this country. A light went on in my head, and I planned a similar activity for the next day. As the reading students filed into the room, I waited until they were all seated and told them that I'd been unhappy with the way the class was going. This caused a sigh, and they all took the slumping posture of students who know they are about to be chewed out by an authority figure. I said that I considered it my fault (faces shot up all over the room) and that I realized I had been too rule oriented and needed to lighten things up (suspicion rippled in their eyes). I suggested that instead of getting right into our regular work, we should play a game. I had everyone stand up and form a large circle around the room. Meanwhile, I pulled a beach ball out from behind my desk. Without giving any directions, I threw the ball at a student. He looked at me, puzzled, but I just smiled and said, "Go ahead!" He shrugged his shoulders and threw the ball at another student. Ignoring the comments about my sanity, I would arbitrarily point at a student and command him or her to sit down. I continued to do this after every few tosses of the ball, and soon there was only one boy left standing. I congratulated him on being the winner and asked him if he wanted to play again. He told me that this was the most ignorant game he'd ever played. I looked hurt and asked him why—I'd had fun. He pointed out that no one knew what to do, they were all just throwing a stupid ball. Another chimed in that there was no winner because they didn't know what I expected. I looked confused and asked what they meant. Bless his heart, one of the most rebellious students in the class shouted out, "We couldn't play right because there were no rules." The last word kind of died on his lips because even though he was one of the most famous behavior problems in the school, he was also very smart. I grinned and innocently asked, "So, you're saying that for a group of people to really have fun, there need to be some guidelines?" The point was quickly taken, and we had a good talk about the rules of my class and the logic behind them. As students got up to go to their groups, I heard one of them say, "I told you she was tricky."

Your class needs rules, but they have to be **your** *rules, based on what will create order in your room and enhance the learning experience.*

Your class needs rules, but they have to be *your* rules, based on what will create order in your room and enhance the learning experience. In my school, every teacher is required to submit an assertive discipline plan to the vice-principal at the beginning of the semester. New teachers are given a sample copy to use, and it amazes me how many of them just copy down the generic rules and consequences and turn those in. Granted, there are some tried-and-true rules that work well, like "Come prepared to work." That covers a lot of territory, from bringing supplies to paying attention. But only an inexperienced teacher would put "No talking" on a rule sheet. That right there is a set-up for failure.

How do I know? Well, let's go back to my best training ground for teaching—my old high school. I once had a teacher who taught English and home economics, and unfortunately for her, I was in both classes. This woman gave the impression of being nervous and angry, and she definitely did not understand the nature of control. I figured I had her sized up within the first 10 minutes of class, and she seemed like fair game. She had yelled at several students already, including me, and I knew she'd be an easy mark. As expected, she sat us in rows and she stood at the front. I used my usual strategy of sitting in the back of the class and hiding behind someone with big hair. This gave me a lot of leeway. She had the rules of her class posted on the front chalkboard, and the minute I saw "No talking" and "Do not get up out of your seat," I knew I was home free. The first time she turned her back to write something on the board, I tossed my pen about 3 feet from my desk, then waved my hand frantically in the air. When she turned around, she eyed me with disgust and asked what I wanted. I smiled and innocently asked her to please come pick up my pen for me because I was just trying to follow her rules and I couldn't ask the person next to me because we couldn't talk and I couldn't get it myself because we couldn't get out of our seats and would she please get it for me now? The class froze as her eyes narrowed and the blood started rushing to her cheeks, but she knew I had her. Glaring at me, she marched to the back of the room, picked up my pen, and slammed it on my desk. I smiled my most angelic smile and thanked her profusely. As she made her way back to the front, I tossed the pen 3 feet in the other direction. When she turned around to continue her lecture, there I was, waving my hand again. By now her voice was cracking when she asked what I wanted this time. I acted all flustered and said I didn't know what was wrong with me, maybe I was just so excited to be back in school or something, but I dropped my pen again and would she please come get it for me because I couldn't talk and I couldn't get out of my seat. That did it. She screamed, "Come with me, young lady!" and marched me down to the principal's office. She told the principal that I was acting up in class, and he asked me to tell him what I'd done. I looked puzzled and said, "I don't know, I was just trying to follow her rules. She told us we couldn't talk or get out of our seats and I dropped my pen and asked her to get it for me." He turned to the teacher and asked if that were true. She kind of sputtered, "Yes, no, yes, but no!" What could she say? She made the rules. I spent many hours sitting in the hall outside of her class as the semester progressed, but I didn't care. She thought she was punishing me, but I was thrilled that I didn't have to sit and listen to her.

Here are some rules for making up rules. First, go back to your vision and the organization of your class and think about what behaviors would inhibit learning—anticipation is everything. Second, physically set up your class to avoid problems before they get there. Spread the students out as much as you can, and allow for unobtrusive movement in the room. Third, make sure that whatever consequence you choose for breaking a rule makes sense, and make sure you're willing to enforce it. Never threaten. Fourth, design a number of activities to help the students develop a sense of community about your class. Students are not as likely to act inappropriately if they feel they are important members of a team with common goals. Finally, spend some time demonstrating to your students why you have the specific rules in place, how the consequences are logical, and what the rewards will be. The students should definitely have the idea that you have rules in your class, not for some false sense of power, but to simplify things and to eliminate chaos. The rules will help them.

I mentioned earlier that one of the hardest things about being a teacher is that you are a constant role model. When you are dealing with your students, you are showing them how to solve problems. You can talk all you want, but they will pay attention to what you do. When you yell and scream at a class, do not be surprised when they yell and scream back at you. If you show them no respect, don't be surprised when they show you none. A teacher who controls a class through threats and accusations had better never turn her back. This kind of power is no power at all. All of us can physically make a student do something—we may have to call in a bigger teacher or an administrator—but there's no trick to making a kid shut up and sit down. It's keeping them there that's difficult. If I want to get out of working in your class, I'll just kick up dust and distract you. That teacher who dragged me to the office so many years ago thought she won, but I did. I successfully delayed her lesson for at least 20 minutes and made her look like a fool in front of her students and her principal. Sure, she gave me an F—been there, done that. That's one of the ways I can tell a teacher is not very good at what she's doing—she has a high percentage of Fs in her grade book. How hard is that? What's difficult is to have a high percentage of students succeeding. Can you think of another business in the world where workers can fail to turn out half of their product and keep their jobs? Only in education. Failing a student is not a sign of power, it's an admission of defeat. I do not believe in giving away passing grades, because that is also a sign of false power. But over and over I see new, as well as experienced, teachers using grades to punish students. Kids who are really behavior problems probably have a string of Fs on their belts—it means nothing to them. Many of them wear the failing grades with pride and are so out of control at home that your threat doesn't even faze them.

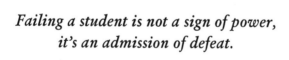

*Failing a student is not a sign of power,
it's an admission of defeat.*

One of our main goals as teachers should be to help students learn self-discipline, and we can't accomplish this if the only control we understand comes from the person in the position of authority. I have a way of making my students understand the true nature of power. I pick the biggest guy in the group and tell him that I can force him to stay in my class. The kids kind of chuckle when I tell the student to try to leave but that it will be impossible because I'm between him and the door. I stand behind the kid and push down on his shoulders and tell him in a strained voice, "OK, now try to leave—you can't do it because I'll hold you back." Everyone laughs when the student easily throws off my hands and heads for the door. I act stunned and ask the group what went wrong. They quickly point out that he was bigger and stronger and wanted to leave. I nod and say, "All right, physical force didn't work, let's try something else." This time I sit down next to the boy, tell him that I will spend the next few months doing everything in my power to help him succeed in his goals, that I am really glad he's there, and that I've got all sorts of exciting and interesting things to teach him. Then I ask if he'd like to stay. He always says yes, and I point out that no one in the room could force him to leave now because he wants to be there. That is true power and the strongest kind of control.

Eliminate a large percentage of behavior problems by having a logical, meaningful answer to "Why do we have to do this junk?"

During the first week of a class, I spend about 20 minutes every day discussing the rules, consequences, and rewards of the class. I have a list of general rules that I submit on the assertive discipline form, and these go home to be signed by the parents. Right now the five rules are as follows:

1. Be on time.
2. Come prepared to work and stay on task.
3. Don't disturb other students.
4. No food or drinks in the room.
5. Know why you are doing an assignment.

Do you see how it is possible to enforce "Don't disturb other students" rather than falling into the "No talking" trap? Students will talk in class—you want them to. What you don't want is that their talking disturbs others and inhibits the learning process. True, this is a judgment call, but that's why they pay you the big bucks. I have known students who were put in detention because they leaned over and asked their neighbor what page they were on. There's a big difference between this and a kid talking so loud that no one can hear what anyone else is saying. My students don't like the fourth rule about no food or drinks because many teachers allow them to do this. To be honest, if I were in someone's class, I'd like to have the option of having a drink on my desk, and I tell my students that. The reason I've banned these things is because of the computers. Students always swear to me that they will never, never take their drinks anywhere near the computers, but it happens every year. After one student accidentally spilled his soft drink on a keyboard, I called it quits. The students usually accept this because it makes sense, and I also use this rule as a reward sometimes. I have a small refrigerator in my room and if a class is working particularly well for the first couple of weeks, I give them the privilege of putting their drinks in there. They have to promise to quietly go get a drink when they need it, but it can never disturb the groups and the drinks must stay in the refrigerator. Because of the four-period day, the classes are long, and some kids have a hard time making it to lunch. But they clearly understand that this privilege is mine to give or take away, and it's up to them to guard it carefully. The fifth rule seems silly, but students who understand why they are doing an assignment not only will complete the work but are not likely to give you a problem because they see the point of what you're asking them to do. You can eliminate a large percentage of behavior problems by having a logical, meaningful answer to "Why do we have to do this junk?"

I have another set of about 15 rules that describes specifically what I expect the students to do when we work in groups. These include never even giving the appearance of sleeping, not playing games like Solitaire on the computer, and having all of their work ready when their group shifts to meet with me. I explain the logic of these rules, and we practice them for several days. I point out how the entire system is designed to ensure that the small group I'm working with will get my undivided attention for the short time I see them every day. The rules benefit them because one third of the time they will be in the special group at my table.

The consequences for breaking the rules in my class are the same for all but being tardy. That's a general school rule, and we follow the schoolwide consequences—three tardies equal 1 day absent. For all of the other rules, I give a verbal warning, quickly and quietly reminding them of what they should be doing. If they ignore that, I ask them to copy out the group rule that are stapled in their folders. This covers about a page of typing and is just annoying enough that they don't want to do it. This write-off has to be turned in at the beginning of class the next day. If not, the write-off is doubled, and if they should fail to bring that in, they go to detention until the write-off is completed. This series of consequences is pretty logical and easy to enforce.

One of the best ways to eliminate discipline problems is to have a reputation as a good teacher who tries to make learning enjoyable but who will do what she says she is going to do.

What are the rewards for following the rules? They get to be in my class. I know this sounds conceited, but one of the best ways to eliminate discipline problems is to have a reputation as a good teacher who tries to make learning enjoyable but who will do what she says she is going to do. When the special education teachers are meeting with parents and students to plan for next year, they often say that if the student is very good, he or she may get to be in Mrs. Gill's class next year. I'm one of the few teachers in the school who doesn't mind working with kids with special needs and who will not make excuses for them. I also inherit many younger brothers, sisters, sweethearts, and friends of former students. They tend to be predisposed to take my class. I don't believe in giving movies or free days as rewards in that these have been overused. I tell the students that their main rewards will be that authentic learning will occur in this class and everything we do will be designed to make them successful in the future. You'd be surprised how effective this is.

When I review the rules on the third day, I role play to make sure that everyone understands exactly what will happen when we break into groups the following week. From the minute they walk in the class, I pay close attention to the kids with attitudes or the ones who overtly call attention to themselves. Even though I don't know them yet, these kids are pretty easy to spot. I tell the students that we're going to go over the rules and consequences one more time to make sure there are no misunderstandings, then I innocently pick one of the potential troublemakers. "Let's say it's next week and everyone is in groups, working away. I'm up at the board getting ready to work with my group. I turn around and (gasp) Joe is sitting there talking with Julie! He's supposed to be on the computers! I'm stunned but I figure he just lost track of the time. I say, 'Joe, you need to get on the computers,' and naturally he smiles, gives me a nod, and gets right to work. He's a great guy. But let's pretend, and I know that this would never happen, but let's pretend that Joe is just having a really bad day and I look up again, and he's *still* sitting there talking to Julie. I can barely believe my eyes I'm so shocked. I say, 'Joe, you need to copy out the group rules stapled in your folder'—I figure he just forgot what he was supposed to do and it will help him out." Then I turn to the class in general and ask, "When I give Joe the write-off, what does he say?" This usually causes general snickers because Joe probably has a history of fighting with teachers, but I break in. "He says, 'Thank you, Mrs. Gill, thank you for giving me this write-off, because you told me that if I ignored your verbal warning, that's what would happen—I even signed a paper agreeing to it—so I want to thank you for being the kind of person who does what she says she's going to do—the kind of person I can trust—bless your heart!' " By now the class is howling, including Joe, but the point is made. There's no arguing when a teacher asks a student to fulfill the consequence of breaking a rule because the student agreed to it ahead of time to stay in the class, and the teacher said that this is what she would do.

The next day, we'll role play again using a different student, and we practice doubling the write-off and heading on down to detention. Again I point out that the student will probably be thanking me profusely as we walk down the hall to the office because I'm the kind of person who keeps her word. At the end of the week, they take a quiz on the rules, and this is the first grade of the semester. Most students get a perfect score, which lets me know that they understand completely what I expect. When I hand back the tests, I can clear up any confusion, and by the time we break into groups the following week, the class runs pretty smoothly.

Just as I don't mind stopping at a traffic light, most students understand that rules are designed to protect them and to create an optimum learning environment.

I rarely take a student to the office—once a year at the most. When I do, the student is in some serious trouble, because it's such a rare occurrence. There are teachers in my school who take an average of one student to the principal per class period. I'm not sure if they do this to scare the students or to get out of embarrassing situations, but it's a huge mistake. It sends two negative messages to two very important groups of people. One, it gives the administrators the impression that the teacher cannot handle his or her students. Two, it lets the students know that the teacher is not the bottom line, it's the administrators who count. I handle almost all of my disciplinary problems myself—the students know it's between the two of us and it will be solved. I do ask advice from the counselors or other teachers to find out background information that may give me a clue as to why a student is acting up in class.

When creating a discipline plan for your class,

1. Anticipate possible problems ahead of time.

2. Create an internal system that allows the students to control most of their own behavior.

3. Be sure your rules are logical and can be enforced.

4. Spend quite a bit of time reviewing the rules and consequences so there is no doubt in anyone's mind what you expect.

5. Do what you say you will do every time in as matter-of-fact a manner as possible.

Just as I don't mind stopping at a traffic light, most students understand that rules are designed to protect them and to create an optimum learning environment. The sixth commandment of good teaching? Thou shalt be fair and prepared for problems before they get there.

7

Thou Shalt Use
Some Common Sense

I've spent a great deal of time telling you about the very specific set of rules and consequences I've designed for my class. I have to run a pretty tight ship because of the short amount of time I have to teach each of the groups. However, you are in a people business and stuff happens. There are times when you will have to make a judgment call based on old-fashioned common sense. There's always an exception to every rule, and you have to be able to read a situation quickly enough to defuse it before it gets out of hand. By working with your students as individually as possible, you can get pretty good at separating the reliable kids from the players.

There are very few times I will allow a student to sit and do nothing in my class. The kids just know that they have to work all period long because that's what I expect. But every once in a while a student will come in who is obviously agitated and at the breaking point. Something may have happened at home or in the last class, and this kid is ready to blow. If I see this, I'll sit next to the kid while the rest of the students are moving around getting into the groups. I'll try to get her to tell me what is wrong, but sometimes she won't talk or—even worse—she'll scream at me. Right then I have to make a decision. I hope I know enough about this student to guess what's wrong. Based on my instincts, I'll take the student into the hall to talk, take the student to the office to talk to someone, or leave her alone to cool down. The one thing I know I *won't* do is take her anger personally. This child may scream that she hates me, but unless I've done something on purpose to make this kid mad, I'm not going to react to the words. This is just misplaced rage and I'd be a fool to buy into it by losing my temper, too.

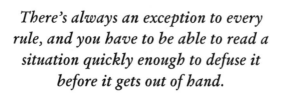

There's always an exception to every rule, and you have to be able to read a situation quickly enough to defuse it before it gets out of hand.

Remember, I'm the role model. I'm not going to show the students the same respect they show me, because I'm the adult—I'll show them far more respect so that they may learn by example. Sometimes students will tell me that I give them too much work or they don't feel like doing anything. I could tell them to sit down and shut up or I'll flunk them. I guess that's one solution. But I usually say, "I give you a lot of work because I care about you. If I didn't respect you, I'd let you sit there and do nothing." I'm the one who sets the tone for the class and treats them better than I expect to be treated.

Another tool in my arsenal is a fine-tuned crap detector. I describe this to the students as a little alarm inside me that goes off when I hear something that doesn't add up. I tell them that this is one of the most powerful resources they can develop to help them in just about any situation they're likely to encounter. As the semester progresses, I'll call a group up to work with me and someone won't have her work done. This person will begin an elaborate story about dogs and homework and a best friend's abandoned car. I'll listen politely, then toward the end I'll look startled and say, "Did you hear that?" The kids will start looking around. I'll turn my head toward the student and say, "Yep, beep, beep, beep, my crap detector just went off." Usually, everyone starts laughing, including the kid with the excuses. A few years ago, one of my students gave me a headline he'd torn out of the newspaper. It said, "The Best Crap Detector in the USA." I proudly pasted it to the front of my roll book and sometimes all I need to do is hold it up and point to it.

Many of your students will have developed some pretty clever games over the years to outwit teachers.

Another book I find very useful is *Games Students Play* (1972) by Ken Ernst. Many of your students will have developed some pretty clever games over the years to outwit teachers. I know I was a major player in high school. One I see all of the time is called "Uproar." It goes like this. A student demands to leave the room at an inappropriate time to go to the restroom. The teacher tells the student no. The student goes berserk, screaming and yelling and creating such a fuss that the teacher lets her go just to get her out of the room. Even if the student is not allowed to leave, the teacher makes a mental note that this kid can create quite an uproar. The next time the student makes an unreasonable demand, the teacher gives in to avoid the scene that's sure to follow. This is probably how that student has been training teachers for years. If you spot an Uproar player, never get into a confrontation with her in front of the whole class. Make one of those quick decisions to ignore it right then or take the student into the hallway. When you get the student alone, call her on her game. Tell her without a trace of anger in your voice that you didn't realize that she was an Uproar player and you're glad you found that out. Smile and nod knowingly when you tell her that you recognize that this is how she's controlled teachers for years, but luckily for her, she's finally found a teacher who understands this game and won't play. Quickly explain why you wouldn't let her leave the class and tell her how you'd like her to handle the same situation in the future. Before you return to class, tell her you're glad she's there, but because you have so much you're trying to accomplish, you just can't have any outbursts like that. This may sound naive to you, but it really works. Remember to handle all discipline problems as matter-of-factly as possible.

Because you're learning to anticipate problems before they occur, you need to develop a simple system that will allow students to leave your class to use the restroom. This may sound ridiculous, but I've noticed that this becomes one of the biggest fights that brings an angry teacher and an angrier student to the principal's office. Refusing to allow students to use the restroom during a 90-minute class is setting yourself up for some serious battles—with parents as well as students. It is almost impossible to tell whether or not a student really has to go, so don't even play that game. I taught for a year next door to a new teacher who was having a horrible time making his students behave. I could literally hear desks being thrown against the wall, and I went over a couple of times, but it embarrassed the teacher so much that I stopped doing it. I offered to help in any way I could, but the teacher was afraid to let anyone know how much trouble he was having because he thought it would cause him to lose his job. He was fired anyway. In a desperate attempt to control his students, he forbade anyone to leave the class under any circumstances. In his defense, he had students leaving four and five times within an hour to "use the bathroom." He told them that they had abused the privilege, so he was taking it away. I was horrified to learn later in the year that one student had urinated in the corner of the room because he said he couldn't hold it any longer. This shows how out of hand things can get when a teacher creates a rule that can't be enforced.

In my class, the students are free to leave the class once per period. I don't ask them where they're going, but they know they have to follow the regular school rules. I leave the hall pass on a counter by the door. They have to sign out, stating where they're going, when they left, and when they returned. I tell them that they cannot leave when their small group is working with me. The only other requirement is that they enter and exit so quietly that no one notices. If they cause a disturbance, they forfeit the privilege for a week. It works pretty smoothly, and it's rare that a student abuses the system. The best advice I can give is to pick and

choose your fights. Arguing about whether the students legiti-
mately need to use the restroom is not one I choose to take on.

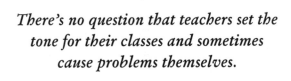

There's no question that teachers set the
tone for their classes and sometimes
cause problems themselves.

It's been my experience that people have a great deal of control over how others react to them. There's no question that
teachers set the tone for their classes and sometimes cause problems themselves. Many years ago, I read a book called *Transac-*
tional Analysis in Psychotherapy (1961) by Eric Berne, the author of
Games People Play. In this book Berne describes a system of behavioral modification called transactional analysis (TA). I found this
especially helpful in developing my instincts for dealing with students. In fact, I teach a mini-unit in TA to my students because it's
so helpful in explaining why people respond to us so differently.
According to TA, each of us has learned how to be a parent, an
adult, and a child by observing the behavior of the significant people in our lives. I tell my students that from the moment they are
born, a little tape recorder goes on in their heads. We record on
these tapes, without evaluating, what it is to be a parent by watching our parents, what it is to be an adult by watching the few we
may run into, and we experience naturally what it is to be a child.
We all have a part of us that reacts like a Critical Parent, a Nurturing Parent, an Adult, a Submissive Child, a Rebellious Child, and
a Free Child. Depending on the personalities of the significant
role models in our lives, we may have more of one than another.
For example, a student who was abandoned or poorly cared for as
a child will not react very often in a Nurturing Parent manner because that's just not something he or she learned when growing
up. Someone who grew up under the thumb of a Critical Parent either learned to be submissive to survive or possibly fought back in

a rebellious manner. And that person will tend to act in the same critical manner as a parent.

I try to get students to analyze themselves and focus on how they most often react to other people. I also point out that many of these "transactional states" are symbiotic. A Nurturing Parent loves to deal with a Submissive Child. Think how this works in a classroom. Teachers who choose to control their students through threats and constant put-downs, the modus operandi of the Critical Parent, will naturally hook into the Rebellious Child in many of their students. Ultimately, the teacher is the one who fuels the conflict by not understanding what is going on. There is no way I'm going to get into a head-on confrontation with a Rebellious Child. I may win a few battles, but I'll surely lose the war. In the same manner, I'm not about to stay in my Nurturing Parent when dealing with my students. Even though this may bring out their submissive natures, it also makes them dependent on me and, therefore, they remain in a childlike state. The logical place to stay in most of our relationships at school is in our Adults. This is the part of us that makes decisions based on the best information available. It tends to bring out the Adult in the students. I would encourage anyone who deals with people on a regular basis to read Berne's book. It was one of those trendy philosophies that sweep through the schools on a regular basis that has actually worked for me for many, many years.

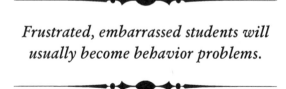

*Frustrated, embarrassed students will
usually become behavior problems.*

Sometimes it seems to me that most of the people who become educators were also the top students in their schools. They were the kids the teachers loved because they were so quiet and well mannered and always had their work done on time. Some of these students go on to become remarkable teachers. However, I've noticed that teachers who never had to struggle to learn or to control their behavior tend to have very little tolerance for the students who do. We may have loved math when we were young, but there are students who find it so baffling and frustrating that they will do whatever they can to keep the teacher from talking about it. As teachers, we have to be sensitive to the fact that few of our students will learn in the same manner as we, and we have to learn to accommodate for these differences. Frustrated, embarrassed students will usually become behavior problems. You need to develop a set of rules by which to run your classes, but sometimes you will be called on to make a decision based on your instincts rather than the normal solutions. The seventh commandment of good teaching? When making choices that will affect your students, thou shalt use some common sense.

8

Thou Shalt Be
Open-Minded and Flexible

Teachers are natural-born leaders. They have to be. But this is why most faculty meetings are such unpleasant experiences. It isn't just staying after school for an extra couple of hours; it's that the room is full of highly opinionated, pushy people who are used to telling others what to do. In all human beings, the quality that is our greatest strength can also be our greatest weakness. It's a fine line between being decisive and being overbearing; between being in charge and being a martinet. When the bell rings and the door closes to the classroom, we're the boss. One of my favorite things about teaching is that no one is looking over my shoulder telling me what to do. The quality of what goes on in my classroom is solely in my hands.

However, I don't teach in isolation. I am part of a community of teachers, and I'm responsible for that group as well. I constantly wrestle with the impulse to stay in my room and ignore the rest of the world. I'll pass by a classroom where the students are obviously out of control and the teacher is struggling. What I most want to do is turn my head and move on. But at my best, I realize that all of the students in the school are my students and that I have an obligation to at least offer to help.

Teaching can be the loneliest profession in the world. When I first began teaching in a middle school in Tennessee, the principal handed me a roll book, a key to my room, and wished me luck. I didn't even know how to take roll and that we teachers would be expected to buy most of our supplies, like chalk. Except for one advanced English class, I struggled through that year, and no one on the staff paid any attention. I was too embarrassed to admit I was having problems because I thought that would make me appear incompetent. My family had just moved to the area from California, and I didn't know a soul. It was the closest I've come to quitting the profession. I had a terrible year because no one offered to help and I didn't ask. Most of the teachers I know have had similar experiences and tend to be very nice about looking out for a newcomer.

I am part of a community of teachers, and I'm responsible for that group as well. I constantly wrestle with the impulse to stay in my room.

On the other hand, keep in mind that we teachers are also an opinionated lot who will offer advice even when it isn't requested. One of the main things I try to remember when I attempt to help someone is that we do not all teach in the same way. Schools are filled with all types of personalities and styles. I think I do a pretty good job in my classes, but I have had students who I feel gained little from being in my class. Either they couldn't handle the freedom incorporated into the setup of my system or they found my earnestness obnoxious. They responded far better to a teacher who sat the students in rows and lectured for most of the period. We all have different teaching and learning styles, and we should honor those. The bottom line is whether your style accomplishes your goals.

One of the biggest traps you can fall into as a teacher is to spend even a small amount of your time worrying or griping about what the teachers down the hall are or aren't doing. First, unless they request your input, it's none of your business. However, if their classes are so chaotic that they disturb your class, that's a different story. The first step would be to speak to the individual teachers, explain the problem, and offer any assistance you can. The second step would be to talk to an administrator about the problem. But this is only if what other teachers do interferes with what you are trying to do.

I have been elected to serve on our Faculty Advisory Committee for years, but I usually refuse. This committee is chosen by the other faculty members to present their concerns to the principal in regular monthly meetings. The idea behind it is to save time, and it also allows a teacher to bring up a sensitive issue anonymously. I used to think of this committee as a powerful force to help steer the school toward a collective vision. In reality, it was usually a rather lengthy gripe session. Each member took turns presenting a list of suggestions from the faculty at large. Ninety percent of these suggestions were either complaints about another faculty member or gripes about situations that were unsolvable due to money constraints. Very few were suggestions or solutions. I stopped participating in this process when I realized that no one was really interested in seeking a solution—it was just a lot of negative energy that was harmful to the morale of the school. Earlier I encouraged you to ask when you need something, but be careful what you ask for because you might get it. For example, some of the teachers in my school spend an inordinate amount of time worrying about what other teachers wear to school. At one point, they demanded that the principal do something about these "unprofessional" colleagues, so the principal offered to set up a very rigid dress code for all teachers. These same teachers were outraged—they didn't want someone dictating what they could or couldn't wear—they mostly wanted to complain. Years ago, I heard a story about a 2-year-old boy, sucking on a pacifier, who was sitting next to his mother. The mother was talking with a large group of women who were planning a party. One of the women kept staring at the boy and finally said, "What in the world are you doing sucking on that pacifier, a big boy like you? That's for babies." The little boy took the pacifier out of his mouth, looked the woman straight in the eye, and said, "Hurts you?" I can't tell you how often this saying runs through my head when I'm listening to teachers complain about one another. I want to ask, "Hurts you?"

*We have to learn to pick and choose
our battles.*

Every year we have a summer faculty meeting during which we discuss plans for the following school year. Every year someone brings up the sorry state of student dress and demands a strictly enforced dress code. This usually results in an hour-long debate over the finer issues such as how baggy can pants be before they're outlawed? How short is too short for a skirt or top? The trouble is that most of these teachers can't define their terms. When I first moved here, I was surprised to hear that boys were not allowed to wear tank tops, but girls were. In my first faculty meeting, I naively asked what was wrong with tank tops and was told that some of the teachers just couldn't stand to see underarm hair. I didn't know how to respond to that, it seemed so ridiculous. We have to learn to pick and choose our battles, and a student dress code is one that screams for common sense. The other teachers know that I pay very little attention to what my students are wearing because I'm looking so hard at their faces to make sure they're understanding what I'm saying. They'd have to have on something pretty outrageous for me to notice.

This debate has gone on so long that when the dress code issue is brought up in a meeting, everyone turns to hear me declare my ultra-radical, bleeding-heart opposition to strict rules that dictate how the kids will dress. But what I say year after year seems like such common sense to me. If what a student is wearing interferes with the learning environment, send that student out of class to change. For that matter, if what a teacher is wearing interferes with the learning environment, that teacher should change. That's it. Sure, this requires judgment calls, but that's why we're the highly respected professionals we're paid to be. I personally would never even notice whether students have on hats in my class unless the brim covers their eyes. If that were the case, I'd tell them to take it off. This is not a big problem. But I have known teachers to waste half a class period up in the office with a student who may or may not have on baggy pants. One of the most disgusting scenes I've observed as a teacher was two male administrators on their knees in front of a 16-year-old girl measuring the length of her skirt. A girl's skirt is too short if it is so distracting that the other students or the teacher cannot concentrate in class.

Remember that the vast majority of the kids in our schools are pretty reasonable, good people.

As we get older, we tend to conveniently forget what we were like when we were young. Everyone of us wore or wanted to wear something that was against an authority figure's rules. Teens are dominated by fads, and the way they dress is an attempt to illustrate for the world who they think they are. I don't advocate allowing students to wear gang colors or anything that could harm anyone. One of our main goals in a school is to provide a safe learning environment, and we must react swiftly and decisively when it comes to protecting our students. But we also need to remember that the vast majority of the kids in our schools are pretty reasonable, good people. Just as it's a huge mistake to punish an entire class for the misdeeds of a few, it's wrong to force all of the students to follow rules set up to punish a few bad seeds. We have to be a little open-minded about people who dress and act differently from ourselves. People should be judged by their actions, not their appearances. People should be judged by the end result, not necessarily by how they got there.

We're in a people business, and we have to remain flexible to survive. Another of my favorite things about teaching is that every 90 minutes everything changes. A whole new set of students comes in with a variety of social, religious, racial, and political backgrounds. If teachers become bored with their jobs, it may be because they've focused so hard on teaching a subject that they've forgotten that they're really teaching students. Not too long ago, a student in one my classes was killed in a car accident. Former students of mine have died before, but never while they were a member of my class. The young man was killed because he and his friends had been drinking. He was by no means a top student—Joe had been involved in gangs and had just returned from the alternative school because he'd been caught smoking on campus so many times. He had a learning disability and an extremely short fuse. To top it off, he was hyperactive, which had caused some real headaches for many teachers. But in my experience, he was kindhearted, funny, and great with computers. He and I got along because he knew I liked him and I would not allow him to behave inappropriately in class.

They kept Joe on a life support system for 2 days after the accident. As I was leaving school on that Monday, the front office secretary called to let me know that Joe had died. I knew that the next day would be difficult not only because I felt terrible, but because I knew many of his friends would be upset as well. On Tuesday morning, one of our counselors announced over the PA system that Joe had died and asked us to think about him during the moment of silence that begins every school day. This brought a few tears to my eyes, but I started to lose it when a senior who had been in a gang with Joe came into my room, threw his arms around me and started crying. I took him out to the hall and we both cried a little out there. I calmed him down, sent him back to class, and headed to the front office to wash my face. Halfway there, one of the male teachers asked me to go into the girls' restroom because he could hear screeching and loud noises. I found nine girls, some lying on the floor, crying their eyes out. I sat down and tried to talk to them a bit, but they were extremely upset and more girls were joining them. Finally, I asked them to come sit with me in the cafeteria so we wouldn't be blocking the door. By then I was surrounded by about 20 girls and boys, most of whom were crying. I sat next to one girl who was just about hysterical and rubbed her back and talked to her. Just when I had them calmed down, one of the administrators came by and asked what we were doing. I told her that these students had been friends of Joe and needed someone to talk to. She said that unfortunately these things do happen, but it was best just to stay busy and not dwell on them. Then she ordered everyone back to class. I had to physically restrain one girl from attacking her. I told the administrator as calmly as I could that I would sit with these students for a while, but that she needed to send someone from the front office to talk with them. She pressed her lips together and marched off. No one came, even after I sent two other people to ask for help. Finally, I took the group, which had swollen to about 30 students, back to my room. I had a first-period class, I was in the middle of preparing my seniors to write their research papers, and I didn't want to spend my day trying to talk with these kids who weren't even my students. But I also had to be flexible enough to realize that this was an extraordinary situation and the best lesson I could teach that day was compassion.

Period after period, students filed into my room to sit and cry or mourn. During that day I was able to talk to gang members and students who were abusing alcohol and drugs about the likely consequences of their choices. The administrators had just presented a program in the last teachers' meeting about gangs, and we had discussed ways to keep gangs from polluting our school. But not one administrator came down to my room to talk to these kids. They were there—the gang members—and they were in a vulnerable state. The door was open, and no one came. True, these were some of the worst kids in the school. True, they were supposed to be in class, and they were breaking the rules by coming to my room. True, this one incident would probably not change everything, but it could change some things.

We have all heard of the "teachable moment," that magic time when what you are saying is exactly what the student needs (and is ready) to hear. It doesn't happen all of the time, but as a teacher, you have to be flexible enough to grab it. I love teaching because of the combination of left-brain linear, logical work and right-brain creative, intuitive work. As a songwriter, my husband understands this miracle. Often he'll work on a song for several months, fine-tuning it or even changing it completely. But every once in a while, a song will drop into his lap finished—he has to scramble to get it written down before it goes away. I call this the funnel to heaven, and I believe gifted people can access this.

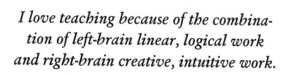

I love teaching because of the combina-
tion of left-brain linear, logical work
and right-brain creative, intuitive work.

Sometimes a lesson I've prepared about writing business letters will evolve into a life-altering experience. Chuck was a student in my senior English class who came with a warning sticker practically stamped on his forehead. He was an infamous trouble-maker and had a volatile temper. He and I understood each other, and I was able to teach him a great deal about word processors and writing. Whenever I teach business letters, I point out how powerful they are as problem-solving tools. I show examples of letters I've written, and I talk about what the letters accomplished. One day, I was sitting in my room during my planning period and the door slammed open. Chuck burst in, and I could see immediately that he was about to explode. He asked me if he could use one of my computers, and I said OK, but don't break it. I could tell he didn't want to talk, so I worked at my desk while he typed away. After much mumbling, he brought a beautifully crafted business letter to my desk for me to read. It turned out that he'd been accused of doing something, not due to any proof, but because of his past reputation. He asked me to show him how to change the format so that he could address the letter to all of the school board members and the superintendent of schools. I was stunned. This was a kid who normally would have slashed the principal's tires or torn down all of the paper-towel holders in the bathrooms. Now he was using something I'd taught him to solve a problem in an adult manner. I couldn't have been more proud.

In another senior English class, I had a group of "skaters" who were constantly clashing with teachers and administrators about the dress code. Teachers would grab them in the hall and yank up their pants or pull off their wallet chains. The students had very little respect for any authority figures, and most were in school only because they'd lose their driver's licenses if they quit. They were a real challenge to teach. As luck would have it, the administrators sent around a lengthy memo outlining a new, rather strict dress code and asked all of the teachers to read it to their classes. This caused general outrage among the students, even those who would never dream of wearing anything out of the ordinary to school, because of the dictatorial nature of the mandate. I overheard one of the leaders of the skaters planning some mayhem for after school. I quietly joined the group and complimented them for playing right into the administrators' hands. They looked at me suspiciously as I told them that causing some destruction to the school would be the best way possible for the administrators to justify their strict rules. "See, these kids are out of hand and we have to crack down on them!"

Michael, the leader, asked me if I thought they should just roll over and take it. I told him that both of the solutions he'd suggested—senseless violence or passivity—sounded pretty chicken to me. He bristled all over and asked me what I thought they should do. I asked the group to tell me whether they were really interested in challenging the dress code or if they just wanted to be a rebel like everyone else. I also asked them if they were willing to put in the extra time and attention that a real solution would require. They assured me that they were serious and tired of being pushed around. So I altered my lesson plans right there and created a unit that would show them how to be proactive rather than reactive. Talk about student motivation. This group of 10 kids who rarely worked in any class became a dynamic organization. They started by interviewing the administrators to get the facts behind the new rules. Then the students developed a questionnaire to poll other students and teachers about their attitudes toward the dress code. Next, the students drafted a report summarizing all of the results and offering suggestions for a compromise. Finally, we invited the principal into the class, at which time Michael orally presented the highlights of the report. When he left, the principal had a professional-looking, 20-page report and a new vision of these kids. He didn't throw out the dress code, but he did make modifications. My students were exhilarated by the experience, and all 10 went on to graduate.

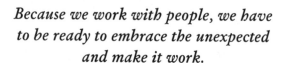

Because we work with people, we have
to be ready to embrace the unexpected
and make it work.

When I first started at this rural Tennessee high school, I was assigned to teach vocational English. The vocational director was an older man, who was also a farmer on the side. He didn't know what to think of this crazy woman from California who spoke and acted so differently. He viewed all of us foreigners with suspicion, and although he was nice, he kept me at arm's length. One day, I came to him with a proposal for a project I wanted to try with my students. He hemmed and hawed and didn't know how to respond. Finally I said, "You know, if we combine some Tennessee 'know-how' with some California 'why not,' we could create the best vocational English program in the state." He loved that idea, and he helped me get my first computers. Some of my colleagues think I'm a laid-back leftover flower child because I do unusual things in my classes and I stand up for the rights of my students. Actually, if they ever watched me teach, they'd see that I'm organized to a fault and tolerate very few inappropriate behaviors. I just understand that because we work with people, we have to be ready to embrace the unexpected and make it work. The eighth commandment of good teaching? Thou shalt be open-minded and flexible because to be successful, you have no other choice.

9

Thou Shalt
Not Work in Fear

———————◦◆●◆◦———————

*Successes have given me the confidence
and the reputation that have earned
me the freedom I enjoy. But my own
best teacher has always been failure.*

———————◦◆●◆◦———————

My entire teaching career has been a series of successes and failures. The successes have given me the confidence and the reputation that have earned me the freedom I enjoy. But my own best teacher has always been failure. A sign that hangs above the computers in my room says, "People who never make mistakes work for people who aren't afraid to." I've made about every mistake in the book, but each one has helped me refine my program, allowing me to rewrite a rule or throw out a lesson and add another. After teaching for 6 years, I decided to put a couch in my classroom so that my students could be comfortable when they were reading. It's a struggle to get some of my students to even open a book, therefore I'm constantly searching for ways to help them associate reading with pleasure. It seemed like a great idea, but even with the best of intentions, students would nod off with a book on their chests. They would also fight over who got to sit on the couch, and I finally decided that the couch was causing more problems than it was worth. I went back to a table and chairs the following year.

You can't expect your first year of teaching to be stress free, and you certainly shouldn't give up just because there were problems. You can allow the problems to defeat you or you can analyze what worked, give yourself credit for what went well, and change what didn't. You need to take chances every year because if you try to please everyone, you'll end up pleasing no one, especially yourself.

I've had teachers sit in my class watching every move I make, and then try to teach exactly like me. It never works. You have to create your own style, your own program, and build enough confidence in it to help you weather the inevitable criticism. There will never be a point in time when everyone is thrilled with what you're doing—it's not possible. I used to moan and groan over the one or two students each year who really hated my class. After listening to this for a while, my husband finally asked, "How about the 98% who loved what you did?" That really helped me to shift my focus from the failures to the successes. A person who pleases everyone is probably teaching within such safe borders that there is no room for growth.

Watch everyone, learn from everyone, but follow your instincts. When designing my classes, I knew I could never live with total quiet or total chaos, so I found a place somewhere between the two that matches my rhythms. Teachers are often guilty of criticizing a colleague who teaches in a totally different style just because it's not how they would do it. Schools would be pretty dull places if everyone taught and learned in exactly the same manner. My daughters have two favorite teachers in common. One was a strict disciplinarian who lectured 95% of the time; the other was a child-centered person who encouraged creativity and risk. The girls loved both of them. These teachers had found their own styles, which freed them to communicate their love for their subjects, and that's all that mattered. Leave yourself open to all suggestions, but use your instincts and experiences to filter out the ones that don't work for you.

To be successful as a teacher, you have to understand the balance of power in the system. When I'm teaching my seniors about succeeding in their chosen careers, I ask them to draw a chart showing the balance of power in our school district. I tell them to place the most important people on top and the least important at the bottom. It amazes me that year after year the kids will put the superintendent at the top and the students at the bottom. They're shocked when I tell them that they have it all wrong. They need to turn their charts upside down to view them correctly. The most important people in our school systems are the students and their parents. They pay our salaries through taxes, and we work for them. The seniors love it when I place the teachers right under the students and often decide to fire someone before the end of the day. (One of my favorite responses to "Why do you make us do so much work?" is "Because that's what you hired me to do. Do you want me to waste your money?") Under the teachers come the counselors and support personnel. Next are the administrators, and finally, we add the superintendent and school board. You may think I'm being facetious, but think about the logic here. The principal's job is to clear the way for me to teach. He works for me in that he removes anything that keeps me from doing the best job of which I'm capable. The superintendent works for the principal in the same manner. She provides whatever is required to make the principal successful in his job. This may seem topsy-turvy at first, but without students, we have no job. We're the only employees in the world who can have dissatisfied customers and keep our jobs. The government is continually threatening to create vouchers that will make everyone view the balance of power in the schools in a different way. Tenure may become a thing of the past.

When you begin teaching in a school, you'd be wise to uncover where the true power lies. Many new teachers live in terror of their principals or supervisors, but administrators are not necessarily the most influential people in a school. During the lesson on the balance of power, I ask my students to name the two people in the school for whom I'll do anything—the two people I most want to keep happy because they can make or break my job. The kids are always surprised when I say that the two people I need the most are the bookkeeper and the head maintenance man. I have found these two to be the bottom line on almost every project I've tried to get off the ground. Sometimes I'll see teachers or administrators treat janitors, maintenance personnel, and secretaries like poor relations, and that is a huge mistake. If angered, these people can cause you more trouble than any principal could hope to do. I'll give you an example. The head of maintenance for my school has worked there since it opened. He moves slowly and doesn't say much. He has little formal education, and some teachers treat him like a servant when they demand his services. The mistake they make is in underestimating his intelligence and not noticing the twinkle in his eye. I've seen him stand calmly while an irate teacher chewed him out about something broken in her classroom. The teacher usually finishes by saying that she wants the problem taken care of immediately! Mr. P just stands there and waits for her to finish. Then he tells her that he will file the necessary forms right away. First, he'll submit the forms to the secretary, who'll get the principal's approval. Then the forms will be sent to the central office, where they'll be processed and returned to him. He hopes, he tells the teacher, he'll get them back before the end of the week. Then he walks off with that twinkle in his eye. The truth is that Mr. P runs the school and can fix anything he chooses when he chooses. The teacher is a fool not to understand how important Mr. P is and to give him the respect he deserves.

The kids are always surprised when I say that the two people I need the most are the bookkeeper and the head maintenance man.

The best way to survive all of the nonsense and politics that occur in any business is to find your people, do everything you can to keep them happy, and operate through them. One of my best friends in my school is a technology teacher. He and I think very much alike, and we will both make it our business to ensure the other's success. My classroom used to be directly above Steve's and he used that to my advantage. We had a supervisor from the central office who would drop by the schools every once in a while, not to encourage and support what was going well, but to sniff out what was wrong. Steve and I would amuse ourselves by driving this man crazy. For example, if Steve ever noticed that the supervisor had entered the building, he'd flip on a rarely used band saw that let everyone in the area know that a negative force was on the loose. We never really had anything to hide, but it was fun.

The best way to survive all of the nonsense and politics that occur in any business is to find your people, do everything you can to keep them happy, and operate through them.

One time this supervisor came into my room to observe me. He was armed with about 20 very detailed forms that, when passed through an elaborate scoring system, would tell him whether I was doing a good job or not. He was a big supporter of the state model for teaching, which specifically timed a teacher as he or she moved through the narrow confines of their idea of the ideal lesson plan. When I saw what he was doing, I told him that I was glad that beginning or poor teachers had such a model to help them out, but that he'd be crazy to ask someone like me to alter a program that had proven to be successful. He became rather agitated, but when he added up all of the numbers, I was one point away from a perfect score. You have no idea how mad that made him. I taught in a completely different style from that in which he had been trained, but it still worked.

There will always be people like this rigid supervisor in your life, and you have to choose how much control to give them. You already know that I'm not afraid of authority figures, but over the years I have learned when to shut up. There are things that go on in school every day that could upset me; I've just gotten better at picking and choosing my battles.

This was a hard lesson I learned when I first started teaching. I was hired to teach reading and English at a high school in central California. Being the new kid on the block, I was assigned to a portable classroom. When I went in to set it up, I discovered that I had only half the number of desks I needed. I went to the front office, straightforwardly introduced myself to the vice-principal, and told him I needed 12 desks right away. To my surprise, his face closed up and he said, "We have many teachers who need many things, I'll put your request on a list, but you may just need to make do." I was stunned and embarrassed because what I wanted seemed so reasonable. As I left his office, it occurred to me that it wasn't my request that was hard to take, it was my manner. I was a young woman with a lot of confidence, but he had perceived me as a pushy female. I waited for a couple of hours, then I went back into his office. This time I acted contrite and confused and told him I really needed his help because I was so nervous about my first job and could he please help out poor pathetic me. I had the desks within 30 minutes. I felt horrible that I had dropped into "helpless female" to get what I wanted, but I also learned that getting the desks was more important than forcing him to treat me with respect. That came later.

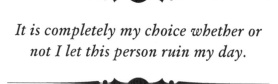

It is completely my choice whether or not I let this person ruin my day.

If someone is doing something to harm a student, physically or emotionally, I will fight that battle. If someone is simply being annoying, I'll just ignore them. Often students will come into my class ready to kill someone because that person had said something they didn't like. My advice is that unless this person is threatening bodily harm to them or their loved ones, don't pay any attention. Students find this very difficult to do, so I offer them my favorite trick. When a person is being ridiculous, yelling at me about a problem I don't own, I visualize him or her as a yappy dog. This allows me to listen and nod, but get no more emotionally involved than I would with a terrier at my ankles. It is completely my choice whether or not I let this person ruin my day.

Most of what goes on outside of your classroom will not be worthy of your attention, but there are fights that you can't be afraid to take on. One year, the principal in my school decided to eradicate drugs from the high school by strip-searching selected students. A surprise announcement came over the PA system instructing us to allow no one to leave the classroom until further notice. We were to wait until a messenger came to our doors to escort certain students to the front office where male and female police officers were waiting. I have always abhorred this type of reactionary method of controlling drug abuse, but I did what I could to calm down my students by pointing out that if they were innocent, they had nothing to worry about. I stood out in the hallway watching the administrators pull students out of the classes. Suddenly, I noticed that the only students being taken to the office were the "hoods" or those from poor families. Without exception, all of the males had long hair and all of the females were dressed in leather or "biker" clothes. I asked another teacher to watch my class, and I ran to the office to find the principal. I asked him to tell me what criteria were being used to select these students. He told me not to get involved, that he knew who the druggies were, and to go back to class. I pointed out that just because students had long hair or didn't look like his idea of "clean-cut," that didn't automatically mean they were using drugs. I told him that if he were really interested in finding the drug abusers, he should pull in a few athletes or some of the rich kids who had the money to spend. He ordered me back to class, and I told him that I hoped he would publish the results of this search so we could all see its effectiveness.

Later that day, I was in my room by myself, and one of the kids who had been taken to the office came in. Carl was a tough kid from an extremely poor family. In fact, his mother had died, and his father bothered to check on his children only every once in a while. Carl had a foul mouth, was overtly racist, and rarely wore clean clothes. He was constantly in fights at school because of his inability to accept any point of view other than his own. I had been trying for months to get him to see how the racist attitudes his father had taught him were simply a pathetic attempt to make someone at the bottom rung of society's ladder feel superior to someone else. I'd had little luck, and I sure didn't think that the current tension in the room could turn into a teachable moment. He stormed over to me and leaned against the counter where I was working. He avoided my eyes, but I could see he'd been crying. I asked him what had happened and he almost started crying again. "Mrs. Gill, they stripped-searched me—they didn't find nothin' because I don't do drugs. I told them that but they didn't care." He slammed his fist against the counter and I told him how sorry I was. The anger was spilling out of him. "They didn't care who I was, I ain't got the money to dress like no rich kid so they just assumed I was guilty." I told him that only foolish or scared people judge others by their appearance. He sputtered, "They just look down on my daddy but I'll get my daddy to come down here and kill 'em all. They don't know nothing about me!" At this point, I said that he must be feeling the same kind of frustration a black person feels when all anyone can see is the color of his skin. Carl looked at me shocked, and for just a moment I saw a shift in his eyes, but it was gone as quickly as it appeared. I spent the next 10 minutes trying to calm Carl down, but I know that for just a moment he knew that the stupid way the administrators handled him matched the ignorance he'd shown toward blacks for years. By the way, after humiliating over 90 students with a strip-search, the administrators found two marijuana seeds in the borrowed jacket of one of the students.

Recently, a new principal ordered a similar lockdown of the entire school, brought in dogs, and searched the purses, backpacks, and pockets of each of the 1,350 students in our school. This time they confiscated aspirin, Midol, cigarettes, lighters, vitamins, and pocket knives. They found no illegal drugs or weapons. We published the results of the search in the school newspaper.

Yes, for reasons that still elude me, my former principal and the English chairperson signed me up to teach journalism. I had never even taken a journalism class in my life, but I was excited by the challenge. We hadn't had a newspaper in our school for many years, and no one wanted to fool with it. To our amazement, my initial staff of 10 produced a 12-page, tabloid-sized monthly publication that regularly sold out within 20 minutes.

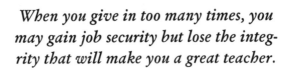

When you give in too many times, you may gain job security but lose the integrity that will make you a great teacher.

During my second year of teaching the class, I was in a meeting where the principal admitted that he had given misinformation to the student body about the number of absences they could accrue before failing a class. At that time, he admitted that he was in violation of school board policy, but to avoid total confusion, he wasn't going to revise his policy until the end of the school year. I saw his point in that it would require a great deal of expense and paperwork to fix the problem in midstream, so I didn't say anything. About a month later, three of my journalism students came to me with the news that two seniors had dropped out of school due to the misinformation. I immediately went to my principal and told him that we would be glad to print a clarification in the next issue of the paper to avoid any further confusion. He ordered me to leave the matter alone. I knew that he was afraid of losing his job over the issue, but I tried to make him understand that this wrong information was actually causing harm to the students. He told me that the newspaper was his and that he had every right to censor what we printed. I told him that he needed to assign someone else to produce a PR sheet for his administration, but that I was assigned to help publish a student newspaper. After a heated debate, I recognized that he would continue to place his best interests over the students', so I got up to leave. When I reached the door, he asked me if I understood what he expected me to do. I turned around and told him that he could always count on me to do the right thing. I knew what was at stake, but we printed the correct information, and the principal never said another word to me about it.

A friend of mine wrote a song in which she describes a poet as a "boat rocker in a deep river," and I think that describes me as well. At the point I'm at right now, it would make my life so much easier to stay in my room and wait for retirement. I've noticed that I don't feel the same fire for the problems that surface year after year—the dress code, the too-complicated record-keeping systems, the scrambling for power. I have a wonderful job and could easily sail through the next few years. But there will always be the student who has been denied her rights or the good teacher who is ready to quit because he feels overwhelmed by the system. I've just learned to be a little better at compromise, and I try more often to make sure I have all the facts before I jump in. I have found a few kindred spirits who encourage me but who aren't afraid to tell me when I'm wrong, and I ignore the rest. New teachers are often afraid to stand up for themselves or their students until they have tenure. However, when you give in too many times, you may gain job security but lose the integrity that will make you a great teacher. It's a delicate balance, and the mentors you choose can help you stay on track. The ninth commandment of good teaching? Thou shalt not work in fear; just be sure you're right and that the battle is worth fighting.

10

Thou Shalt Raise Your Expectations

One of the biggest mistakes we can make as educators is to view students as empty vessels just waiting for us to remove their lids and pour in the knowledge. Wouldn't it be easy if this were true? But the reality is that the students come to us with all levels of skills, experiences, and expectations. Our challenge is to move them all forward, and this can be an overwhelming task.

I believe in "no excuses" teaching. It may be true that kids these days have gotten increasingly difficult to teach. The majority come from broken homes, some live in nightmarish conditions, others view school as a total waste of time. Either because of the changes in the evaluation system or because of the unstable conditions in many homes, I find that I'm working with more and more students with learning disabilities. I can think of a million reasons to believe that these kids are not teachable, but I refuse to do that. This is one area in which I choose to work in ignorance.

When I first started teaching in this small-town high school, a colleague who had lived in the community all of her life asked to see my roll sheets. She knew I was new to the area, and she wanted to help me out. She proceeded to call out the names on my roll, letting me know that this one was from a good family, that one was bad news, this kid was the mayor's son, that one's daddy was in jail. I was horrified and purposely ignored what she was saying. When the students enter my room at the first of the year, they are all the same to me. I pay no attention to what another teacher has to say about a student's potential. I have a good friend in the counseling office who lets me know about any medical or emotional problems that may affect the students' performances, but other than that, I want to gather my own impressions.

One of the ways I know a teacher is headed for burnout city is when she begins to offer more and more excuses as to why her students can't be taught. There's always a reason: overcrowded classes, not enough technology, indifferent parents, lack of funds, hostile students. This is when you need to clearly focus on the things you can do something about and the things that are beyond your control. Teachers rarely accept a student's excuse for being tardy or not turning in homework. They point out that life is not fair and that there will be no excuses when the student gets on the job. We teachers are on the job, life is not fair, and we shouldn't make excuses either. We need to fix what we can and get a little more clever about the rest.

There are three kinds of people: those who make things happen, those who watch things happen, and those who say, "What happened?"

One year, the counseling office put 29 students in my reading lab. I didn't find out about it until the day before school started. I told the counselors that they had to remove 14 students because the reading lab was designed for a maximum of 15. They said it was a computer mix-up, but the students were already scheduled in, and they'd try to fix it for next semester. I told them that they had to make a decision. Did they want me to teach these students to read, or did they want to use me for crowd control? It was up to them. They told me that many teachers had overcrowded classes that year and asked me if I thought I was special. I said yes, and luckily they agreed. I also did everything I could to help reduce the class sizes of the other teachers.

Another sign in my room says there are three kinds of people: those who make things happen, those who watch things happen, and those who say "What happened?" I don't believe in being a squeaky wheel to test my power, but I do believe in setting up the best learning atmosphere possible and then doing whatever is necessary to protect it. I begin each class expecting that all of my students will succeed and that I will do everything within my power to make sure they do.

I believe the worst thing you can do to students is to feel sorry for them. There are no remedial jobs in real life.

In the same manner, I expect a lot out of my students because I believe kids will either live up or down to my expectations. I firmly believe that a teacher can maintain high standards and still have a very small percentage of failures. I also believe the worst thing you can do to students is to feel sorry for them. There are no remedial jobs in real life. When the kids face the world of work, no one will let them do less than what is required because of pity. There have been times when other people thought I was being mean to students by holding them to the same standards as the rest of the class. Robert, a student with Down's syndrome, was placed in my reading lab because he needed to learn to socialize outside of his CDC class. He was 16 years old, and few teachers had required him to do much because he had problems controlling his emotions. Usually, they just let Robert sit in the back of the class and do whatever kept him quiet. When I agreed to let him in my reading class, I told his parents that I would expect him to work just like my other students. They readily agreed, and I spent some extra time teaching Robert to use the computers and operate within the groups of my class. One day I was called to the office, so I told Robert's group that I'd be working with them next and to be ready to go as soon as I got back. When I returned to the classroom,

Robert was on the floor crying and several students were standing helplessly around him. They told me he'd become upset over something and wouldn't get up. I walked over to him, told him it was time to get to work and asked that as long as he was down there, would he mind getting that piece of paper behind that counter? I hadn't been able to reach it myself. Several students looked at me, horrified that I had shown so little concern for this special child. Robert glanced up at me, gave a couple more sobs, but quickly retrieved the paper and joined his group at my table. As the semester progressed, he learned to type and mail business letters and work cooperatively in a group. He and his parents were delighted with his success.

Another student who pulled at my heart was in my senior English class. Linda was a little out of her league, but did not want to take a remedial English class. She struggled through most of her assignments but was willing to go back and correct what was wrong. Midway through the year, she woke up one morning to find her mother dead on the sofa. She had no father and one married brother who was not much support. As you can imagine, she missed a number of school days and was overwhelmed when she returned. I did everything in my power to help her catch up, but she continued to miss days due to depression or illness. When I averaged the final grades for her class, we discovered that she had not passed. She burst into tears and begged me to change her grade like many of her other teachers had done. I told her that she planned to work as a secretary when she graduated from high school and that her writing skills were not even close to what they needed to be. She begged me to think of a way for her to do extra credit work, and I promised I would. When she came to see me the next day, I had a packet of work designed to remediate what she had failed and improve her writing abilities. I told her that most of it needed to be done on the word processor and it had to be completed correctly within 1 week. Her heart sank when she saw the amount of work, but she took it with her. Later in the day, another teacher told me he'd seen Linda crying in the cafeteria because she had so much to do. I know he thought I was torturing this child who had suffered so much already, but I tried to explain that by just handing her a grade she didn't deserve, I'd be doing her a real disservice.

Luckily, Linda rose to the challenge and completed all of the necessary work to pass with a D–. I attended graduation mostly for her, and even though it had been a struggle, she was able to proudly claim the diploma she had earned.

You need to constantly raise your expectations for yourself.

I also believe you need to constantly raise your expectations for yourself. After years of refining, I've been satisfied with the design of my senior English class, but I would never dream of resting there. Just as my students change every year, what is required of them in the "real world" changes. I have to stay up-to-date with materials and technology or I'll be holding my students back. When I was student teaching, I worked under a teacher who was very generous with his materials. I was flipping through a stack of his files and was dismayed to find the masters to several handouts that he reprinted over and over. This teacher had been giving his students the exact same worksheets for 20 years. I'm sure some of it was useful, timeworthy information, but I would challenge his method for two reasons. One, the sheer volume of facts available to students increases exponentially every year, and what will be required of them on the job is in a constant state of flux. Two, one of the quickest roads to burnout is to teach the same thing year after year in the same way. I was terrified when I was assigned the journalism class because it definitely moved me out of my area of expertise. In retrospect, it revitalized me. The easy road is to stay in our comfort zone. It's much more difficult to become a learner again and scramble to stay ahead of the students, but our energy and enthusiasm will be contagious.

At the beginning of every year, our central office distributes a list of the teachers who will be evaluated during that year. This is usually greeted with moans and groans as the teachers anticipate the extra work that will be required. To be honest, I'm not crazy about someone coming into my class to tell me what I'm doing wrong. However, even though I gripe with the best of them, I have never failed to learn something from an evaluation. Sometimes it reinforces my belief in the way I teach. Other times it makes me question and defend what I'm doing. In either case, it helps me to become a better teacher. I'm not so foolish as to passively accept every suggestion the evaluator may make, but I'm also not so foolish as to think that what I do is perfect and cannot be improved. Even when I think a criticism is dead wrong, it makes me go back and look at my system to see why the observer would interpret it incorrectly. If I think my evaluator just missed the point of what I did, I ignore her critique. If I see the point she is making, I incorporate her suggestions into the system.

In the long run, my most useful evaluators are my students. Who better knows the quality of my work? Attached to the final exam for each of my classes is an evaluation sheet. I ask the students to specifically describe the activities we did that were the most and the least useful to them. I also want to know why. I tell them before I hand out the exam that I will tear the evaluation sheet off before I grade their tests and I won't look at it until my final grades are on their report cards. I want them to give me honest feedback that will help me improve my classes, and buttering me up or putting me down will not affect their grades in any way. I pay very close attention to what my students tell me. Sometimes I'm hurt that a unit I was particularly proud of was pretty meaningless to them. Then again they'll surprise me by wanting more of the repetitive work I thought they'd find boring, like vocabulary and spelling exercises. Whenever I run into former graduates, I ask them to tell me about the things we did in class that turned out to be useful to them later on. I never take a negative evaluation personally; that would be like the students who throw fits because they received an F on their tests. An evaluation is nothing more than useful information about someone else's perception of what I'm doing. An evaluation is not what makes a good or bad teacher, it's just another person's opinion. The only people who need to fear evaluations are those who refuse to grow.

As a teacher, you have the power to
change the world one child at a time.

My husband has a philosophy that used to drive me nuts, but I've now come to embrace it. He often says, "Just because something is impossible is not a good enough reason not to try." Despite its awkward wording, it holds much truth. We're the only country in the world that attempts to educate its entire populace. As teachers, we face an impossible job. We are asked to accept every product, no matter how defective, and get it ready to work. We are asked to be calm, intelligent, loving role models day after day, year after year. We are asked to work through the layers and layers of disuse to find the spark that will ignite a student on the quest to discover the meaning of his or her life. We are asked to accept the fact that we will never be paid what we're worth, and many of the miracles we perform will go unappreciated. But as I said earlier, if it were easy, anyone could do it. As a teacher, you are part of an elite group of people who can improve the life of another human being. The tenth commandment of good teaching? Thou shalt raise your expectations for yourself and your students. As a teacher, you have the power to change the world one child at a time.